Proven Resources For Stewardship Promotion

Written and Compiled by
Allan J. Weenink

CSS Publishing Company, Inc., Lima, Ohio

PROVEN RESOURCES FOR STEWARDSHIP PROMOTION

Copyright © 2001 by
CSS Publishing Company, Inc.
Lima, Ohio

All rights reserved. No part of this publication may be reproduced in any manner whatsoever without the prior permission of the publisher, except in the case of brief quotations embodied in critical articles and reviews. Inquiries should be addressed to: Permissions, CSS Publishing Company, Inc., P.O. Box 4503, Lima, Ohio 45802-4503.

Scripture quotations are from the *New Revised Standard Version of the Bible*, copyright 1989 by the Division of Christian Education of the National Council of the Churches of Christ in the USA. Used by permission.

Scripture quotations identified (GNB) are from the *Good News Bible, in Today's English Version*. Copyright © American Bible Society 1966, 1971, 1976. Used by permission.

Library of Congress Cataloging-in-Publication Data

Weenink, Allan J.
    Proven resources for stewardship promotion / written and compiled by Allan J. Weenink.
        p.   cm.
    Includes bibliographical references.
    ISBN 0-7880-1880-9 (alk. paper)
    1. Stewardship, Christian—Presbyterian Church. 2. Presbyterian Church—Finance. 3. Church finance. I. Title.
BX9189.5 .W44   2001
254'.05137—dc21
                                                                                     2001037933
                                                                                                CIP

For more information about CSS Publishing Company resources, visit our website at www.csspub.com.

ISBN 0-7880-1880-9   PRINTED IN U.S.A.

*Dedicated with gratitude to the late
Daniel G. Nicely,
a soul-mate in stewardship,
and
to my esteemed colleagues in ministry
of
the Staff of Lake Michigan Presbytery
and
the Program and Support Staff of
Westminster Presbyterian Church
Grand Rapids, Michigan*

Table Of Contents

Foreword 7

Preface 11

Contributors 13

Part I *Basic Understandings*
Some Stewardship Perspectives 17
Cultivating The Grace Of Generosity 19
The Pastor As A Stewardship Model 21
The Local Church As A Stewardship Model 31

Part II *New Member Training*
The Disciple As A Steward 39
Mission And Stewardship: Fulfilling The Mandate 41
A Time For Reflection 46
Our Philosophy Of Financial Support 49
My Pledge 51
Pledging 51

Part III *Stewardship Sermons*
Neither Poverty Nor Riches 55
Vision 2000 And Beyond:
  What Does Money Have To Do With It? 62
A Tip Or A Tithe 68
Stewardship's Toughest Question 73
All That Is Not Given Is Lost 80
Dispensers Of The Magnificently Varied Grace Of God 87

Part IV *Nurturing Children And Youth*
Introduction To Stewardship For Children 95
The Church School Teacher As A Stewardship Enabler 99
The Youth Budget 104

Part V *Stewardship As Worship, Ministry, And Mission*
    Pledge Dedication Sunday   109
    Now Thank We All Our God   112
    Your Mission Through Your Pledge   113
    Worshiping God   115
    Putting Faith Into Practice   116
    Mission — What It Is   118
    Your Church Involves You   120
    A Poem For Pledge Dedication Sunday   121
    A Hymn For Pledge Dedication Sunday   122

Part VI *Bequests As Blessings*
    The Stewardship Of Bequests   125
    Christian Wills   128
    Mission Through Lending   130
    Sample Trust Agreement   132

Part VII *Inspirational, Informational, And Illustrative Material*
    Some Titanic Thoughts On Small Thinking   139
    To Be Spiritually Fit   141
    God, Where Are You?   142
    Make Mine The Same   144
    Keeping The Pledge Covenant   146
    Compassion Fatigue   147
    How To Celebrate A Church Anniversary   149
    Statements/Reminders/Mission Interpreters   150
    Stewardship Season Humor   152

Foreword

Years ago, about the time I started to grasp ideas and actually puzzle them through on my own, a favorite teacher of mine popped out with the following pair of sentences: "The *beauty* of a profound truth lies in its simplicity. The *mystery* of that same truth beckons through its unending number of practical applications." I was in junior high school at the time. I liked the ring of the two sentences. I relished the sweep of the words and their gentle openness. After all, the teacher was not telling us what to think. She was just inviting us to keep our eyes open. *Look around you*, she seemed to say. *If you find a truth, a really profound one, it will be simple. And once you have found it, well then, you can spend a lifetime discovering what it is about.*

Few statements more perfectly fit that teacher's description of a profound truth than the brief assertion, "For the Christian, stewardship is a way of life." The beauty is right there in the utter simplicity of the expression itself. Point-blank, we hear that stewardship is not a surface reality. It is not simply a programmatic emphasis carried out for a brief time by a few intense and clever folk. At root, and profoundly, stewardship is a way of being. If we hear this much and think about it, we may well say, "Amen!" Wisely, we don't want to mess up the beauty of the expression with yet further words. Just let it be, we tell ourselves. And let the words sink in deeply, where they belong. Stewardship is a way of life. Saying this catches the heart of the matter. In a way, it is enough.

And yet, the mystery beckons. If, for the Christian, stewardship is a way of life, how do we enter upon that way? Where do we begin in our own understanding? Or what fresh insights can deepen the understanding we already have? And when it comes to sharing the goodness of stewardship-living in the community of faith, how do we teach the young? ... those new to the faith? ... even the somewhat jaded? What blessings come, purely as a gift of God, as we grow in the ways of stewardship? And what new forms of stewardship beckon as, through the years, we seek to live as disciples of Jesus? ... as we grow older? ... as we consider such special matters as an anniversary in our community of faith or such personal ones as the legacy we might leave for the blessing of others? The very simplicity of the call to live as stewards points us to the mystery. Yes, we hear the call, the steady invitation. But how, on ever-deepening levels, do we live out the call?

In more than thirty years of ministry, I have never met a person who more straightforwardly lives both the simplicity and the mystery of Christian stewardship than does Allan Weenink. On the matter of stewardship, he is like the botanist who will examine a single flower from all angles, discovering now one property of its life and now another, and then, after what seems to be an aeon of looking, will say, "Ah, and there is so much more to learn!" Or he is like the astronomer who is forever finding fresh signs of beauty in the distant reaches of space. And like the ardent astronomer, or the enthusiastic botanist, or any other person who truly loves the very act of faithful exploration, Allan Weenink shares his discoveries with an infectious joy.

For nearly a decade I have been on the receiving end of that infectious joy. I have watched as, with great devotion and marvelous perception, Allan has helped the laity and clergy of over seventy congregations move ever more fully into the goodness and blessing of living as true stewards of God's abundant gifts. As Associate for Stewardship and Mission for Lake Michigan Presbytery, a regional body of the Presbyterian Church (U.S.A.), he has cultivated the understanding of stewardship in congregations of all sizes and in all manner of demographic settings. And because I came to be a part of this particular presbytery many years after Allan first began his work here, I have from the start seen that his seasoned counsel, his clear theology of stewardship, and his ever-practical suggestions have borne rich fruit. In congregation after congregation, these fruits have included a greater understanding of the call to live as stewards, deeper financial commitment to the mission of the whole Church of Jesus Christ, a rediscovery of the joys of generosity, and a deep sensitivity to the ever-fresh blessings with which God sustains and nourishes the life we share together.

Proven Resources For Stewardship Promotion is, quite truly, the work of an explorer. An enthusiastic explorer. An explorer who, through many years as a devoted pastor and then as a denominational leader, has also become the very best of guides. Through *Proven Resources For Stewardship Promotion*, Allan Weenink is saying, in ever-practical ways, "Come, here are ways that you and others can continuously find joy in the wonderful and all-embracing realm of stewardship-living." Those who read the following pages will indeed find joy, and much spiritual deepening, in their explorations.

Stephen V. Doughty
Executive Presbyter
Lake Michigan Presbytery

Preface

I have always had a passion for stewardship since "the Great Depression days" when I watched my father put aside a tithe every Saturday night. This was not only a time of dutiful discipline but in essence a spiritual experience and an act of worship. That example marked me for life. Giving is an expression of praise. Watching worshipers in Mozambique come down the aisle smiling and singing lustily as they "danced the offering" and presented their gifts in worship, elevated the offering from a routine rite to a celebration of joy. And that marked me too! Duty and discipline, thanksgiving and celebration, have been at the heart of my zeal for stewardship.

Having served on the staff of the Presbytery of Lake Michigan for sixteen years as Consultant for Stewardship and Mission, I conducted countless workshops and seminars. During this period and earlier during 38 years in the parish ministry, I kept searching for new material while refining that which formed the basis for presentations to pastors, sessions, and workshop participants.

Often people would ask me to put in book form some of the material which I developed for use by the churches of the presbytery. Linda Knieriemen, an esteemed colleague, once said to me that younger preachers needed to have access to the accumulated wisdom of pastors who took stewardship seriously. Doris Campbell, Associate for Shared Ministries of the Synod of the Covenant, has also been most gracious in requesting a wider sharing of accumulated stewardship information. With humility, I accept the task.

Through the years I have made no apology for talking about money, mission, and stewardship. It really has become a passion. I hope this book will encourage others to be unapologetic in their zeal.

To the best of my knowledge and resources, I have tried to give due credit for all materials used. If my best attempts have failed, I express regret.

Contributors

The Reverend Anna Kay Baker is a graduate of Union Theological Seminary and School of Christian Education (Richmond, Virginia). She served for a number of years on the staff of the Presbytery of Lake Michigan as Consultant for Christian Education.

The Reverend William A. Evertsberg, Senior Pastor of the First Presbyterian Church of Greenwich, Connecticut, is a graduate of Calvin College and Princeton Theological Seminary. He formerly served as Senior Pastor of the Westminster Presbyterian Church of Grand Rapids, Michigan.

The Reverend Riley E. Jensen, Senior Pastor of the Westminster Presbyterian Church of Grand Rapids, Michigan, is a graduate of Wellmont College and Fuller Theological Seminary. He holds the D.Min. degree from San Francisco Theological Seminary.

The Reverend Linda A. Knieriemen, Associate Pastor of Nurture and Witness at Westminster Presbyterian Church of Grand Rapids, Michigan, is a graduate of the University of Minnesota and Princeton Theological Seminary. She began her professional career as a clinical dietician and holds the Master of Public Health degree from the University of Michigan.

The late Mr. Daniel G. Nicely served for some 25 years as Minister of Administration at Westminster Presbyterian Church of Grand Rapids, Michigan. He began his professional career as a church music director and graduated from Westminster Choir College. He held the Master of Music degree from Westminster Choir College and did further graduate work at Princeton Theological Seminary.

The Reverend Jeffrey D. Weenink, Senior Pastor of the First Presbyterian Church of Bay City, Michigan, is a graduate of Alma College and Duke Divinity School. He holds the D.Min. degree from San Francisco Theological Seminary.

Part I

Basic Understandings

Some Stewardship Perspectives

"In a very real sense every sermon is a stewardship sermon, for it must always be undergirded with the recognition of God's sovereignty and a person's responsibility. The sovereignty of God extends over every aspect of a person's life, including one's pocketbook, and stewardship concerns not only money but a person's whole existence in responsibility to God." (T. A. Kantonen, *Select Stewardship Sermons*, "Foreword." Used by permission from CSS Publishing Co., 517 S. Main St., Lima, Ohio 45802-4503)

* * * * *

"When a church asks for money, it needs to understand itself as inviting people to participate, as finite creatures and means of finite resources, in that Creativity through which all things are made, and made steadily new. Every believer has the right to experience the joy of genuine self-giving which God experiences in every moment of the universe's existence. The church needs a strategy which will allow such joy to come full into being. And there is no better place to begin than with the formulation and securing of the annual budget." (Leroy T. Howe, *The Joy of Giving*, "Church Management," October 1982. Used by permission, Logos Productions, Inc., Inver Grove Heights, Minnesota)

* * * * *

"Christian giving, like the Hebrew's tithing, creates an opportunity to celebrate. We are sharing our 'prosperity' in Christ, believing that all we have is by his grace. We are saved to serve, and we are loved in order to love. To be able to give and rejoice must mean that the giver knows indubitably that love is the ultimate of all the powers of the universe, and that God is love. That is something to celebrate." (Excerpt from *A Present Witness*, © Michael D. Anderson. Reprinted by permission of Morehouse Publishing, Harrisburg, Pennsylvania)

* * * * *

"Giving is an expression of faith. It may be an overt act. But it is also a way of externalizing inner convictions. Faith needs to be objective as well as subjective. The corporate faith of a congregation is demonstrated by what a church does with its money even as an individual's giving is an indication of the reality of that individual's faith. By the same token, an individual is strengthened in the conviction one holds by the attitude, philosophy, and example of one's particular church." (Allan J. Weenink, *The Art of Church Canvass*, p. 130, Keats Publishing Co., New Canaan, Connecticut 06840)

* * * * *

"Giving has always been a mark of Christian commitment and discipleship. The ways in which a believer uses God's gifts of material goods, personal abilities, and time should reflect a faithful response to God's self-giving in Jesus Christ and Christ's call to minister to and share with others in the world. Tithing is a primary expression of the Christian discipleship of stewardship." (*Book of Order* — The Constitution of the Presbyterian Church U.S.A. — Part II — W-5.5004)

* * * * *

"Christian stewardship is the practice of the Christian religion. It begins with the affirmation that God in Jesus Christ calls us to be stewards and the Holy Spirit enables us as stewards. The faith we hold and share is a gift of God. The grace to respond to God in the stewardship of everything is a gift of God. Growth in the stewardship of money is one evidence of growth in the expression of faith." (*A Stewardship Affirmation* — Affirmed by the Presbytery of Lake Michigan, Presbyterian Church U.S.A. — September, 1983)

Cultivating The Grace Of Generosity

1. **Focus on ministry and mission, not your budget.** A budget has little power to motivate members to increased commitment. Celebrate the church's ministry and mission. Show your members how their giving transforms lives and institutions in the name of Jesus Christ. Highlight the growing edge of your ministry.

2. **Be positive — share the good news.** The message that motivates best is the good news of a church alive. Help members see the signs of God at work in their midst. Affirm what is happening in the church as a result of members' commitments and provide a vision of what could happen as a result of increased financial commitment.

3. **Emphasize proportionate giving.** The average member gives between one and two percent of income to the church. Challenge members to pledge a minimum of five percent of income to the church and to build upon that commitment by increasing their giving by at least one percent of income each year, working toward a tithe and more. Build up your disciples, not just your budget.

4. **Visit your members — don't just send letters.** The greatest commitment always is nurtured in face-to-face conversations. As one stewardship leader put it: "Great gifts come from great conversations."

5. **Involve children and youth.** Teaching people to share their time, talents, and material resources is an essential focus of Christian education. A new generation of faithful disciples will not be nurtured unless, and until, we share with even the littlest ones the true joy of giving.

6. **Ask boldly in the name of Christ — don't apologize.** Seeking financial resources for the ministry of Christ and the church is a privilege, not a burden.

7. **Create a year-round program to teach stewardship.** The challenge we face in building disciples is greater than we can address in a few eager words during a fall stewardship campaign. Developing a theology of stewardship in the life of the congregation is a continuing process of nurture.

8. **Preach about stewardship.** The pastor has a responsibility to help develop a theology of stewardship for members of the congregation. Sound stewardship preaching constantly challenges Christians to grow in love-response as part of a distinctive way of life.

9. **Teach new members about stewardship as part of their preparation for church membership.** Prepare an interpretive sheet(s) or brochure indicating the importance of giving as a sacramental experience — the expression of faith through outward generosity.

10. **Thank members regularly for their contributions.** When quarterly statement/reminders are sent, in addition to figures, write an expression of thanks from the church. In addition to giving thanks, interpret for members how their money is used for mission or service in brief remarks: (500 children, youth, and adults use First Church each week for worship, education, fellowship, recreation, and so on." "Your giving makes possible the entire program of First Church." "Our church supports fifteen people in mission and your contributions multiply their ministry of touching lives in the name of Jesus Christ.") (From a stewardship statement by David MacDonald which first appeared in *Vanguard*. I am grateful for permission to use, adapt, and supplement.)

The Pastor As A Stewardship Model

Introduction

"Dr. John Hermann was right on target when he wrote a book for pastors and titled it, *The Chief Steward*. Other persons are involved in stewardship in the local church, of course, and a pastor who tries personally to do everything makes a sad mistake. But the opposite danger is also a serious one — that the pastor may give the impression of a complete lack of concern. If money is never mentioned from the pulpit, for example, the message is clearly conveyed that this is a 'personal' area of life having nothing to do with matters of faith. Or if the mission of the church in community and world is never mentioned, the message is clearly conveyed that mission is not an integral part of life in the faith. Sermons not preached, emphases not made — speak volumes, and members of a church are quick to take their cue from them. If it's not important to the pastor, why should it be so important to us?" (Mark Landfried, *This Service of Love*, Pennsylvania, Synod of the Trinity, 1981, p. 56)

I. Preaching And Teaching

God never assumed that people would discover the joys of giving or accept responsibility for giving without instruction. In the Old Testament, God gave firm instructions about what to give for the tabernacle (Exodus 25:1-8). God also pointed out what to provide for the poor and the stranger (Deuteronomy 15:10-11). Moses, the spiritual leader, was to declare all these things. The prophets were positive in letting the people know they should be giving. "Bring all the tithes into the storehouse ..." said Malachi.

It has been said that there are about 500 references to prayer in the Bible, about 500 references to faith, but more than 1,000 references to one's possessions. Obviously if there are more than 1,000 references to a person's possessions in the Bible, it is important to God. And it is equally important that the subject needs to be addressed more than occasionally from the pulpit. Preaching that involves a theology of stewardship and the spiritual basis for giving is part of pulpit accountability. The Bible gives no hint that God's spiritual leaders are to avoid the mention of money. Money is part of life and life is the pastor's domain.

"John Chrysostom preached stewardship every Sunday. So can we. Our own conviction about stewardship as an essential element of the Christian life gives rise to consistent preaching of stewardship. If stewardship is not a daily part of our own lives, we will find it impossible to preach convincingly and consistently. Part of our own task will be to be self-aware of the ordinary and persistent character of stewardship. 'Know thyself' is a good motto for a preacher as well as for a philosopher." (Patricia Wilson-Kastner, *Preaching Stewardship — An Every-Sunday Theme*, New York, The Office of Stewardship — The Episcopal Center, p. 14, Monograph)

Jesus Speaks About Stewardship

Jesus said more about money than he said about heaven. He used every opportunity to instruct people in the use of the things they possess. To him, a most serious problem in the way of a person's complete relationship with God, was the matter of possessions. Someone once calculated that one-sixth of Jesus' recorded teachings are concerned with the matter of possessions. One-third of all the parables are devoted to that subject.

Jesus, according to the Gospel accounts, spoke five times more frequently about earthly possessions than about prayer. Neither his teachings nor his lifestyle suggests or implies that the material is evil or the spiritual is good. Certainly, he made no apology for preaching and teaching about stewardship and possessions. Quite the contrary; he was explicit, positive, obvious, and to his critics even aggressive in the matter. From our Lord's example we readily observe that this was not a secondary issue nor an optional matter.

Our Lord was vitally concerned in his teaching that those who heard him would respond to the grace of God through gratitude and witness to that love through discipleship. He does not call for mere passible acceptance, but for consecrated action channeled into meaningful service. He confirms his own life mission and preaching with a personal testimony that there is no mistaking his convictions: "My food is to do the will of him who sent me, and to complete his work" (John 4:34). But with confirmation there is also commissioning to those he has chosen: "As you have sent me into the world, so I have sent them into the world" (John 17:18). Stewardship preaching must be re-inforced with one's own positive affirmation and witness.

"One other emphasis in our Lord's teaching on stewardship needs to be sounded, namely, the steward's responsibility. 'To whom much is given, of that person shall much be required.' This is the central thought of the stewardship parables. The entrusted talents must be accounted for. The master of the household will return at an unknown hour expecting every servant to be at the assigned post. The steward who used the master's property for personal ends will be punished. Our Lord's message is never merely sweetness and light. The thought of judgment is always present as a solemn undertone." (T. A. Kantonen, *A Theology for Christian Stewardship*, Philadelphia, Muhlenberg Press, 1956, p. 48)

Paul Emphasizes Stewardship

Paul spoke often and affirmatively about stewardship. He sounded no uncertain trumpet. Paul urged his fellow Christians, with no apology, to give (a) as the Lord had prospered them, (b) regularly, (c) cheerfully, and (d) proportionately. In 2 Corinthians 9:13 (J. B. Phillips) he literally shouts: "... your very giving proves the reality of your faith, and that means that people thank God that you practice the gospel that you profess to believe in, as well as for the actual gifts you make to them and to others."

Paul states emphatically that giving is an expression of faith. It is actually the proof of what one believes or literally a profession of faith. Faith needs to be kept in the heart while at the same time expressed in an "overflowing tide of thanksgiving to God." Therefore, giving may be an overt act. But it is a way of externalizing inner convictions.

Paul emphasized the following biblical motives for giving:
- Give as a response to God's grace (2 Corinthians 8:7; 1 Corinthians 4:7; 2 Corinthians 9:8).

- Give as a response to the example of Christ who gave himself for us (2 Corinthians 8:9).
- Give as a response to human need (2 Corinthians 8:14).
- Give as an expression of thanksgiving to God (2 Corinthians 9:12).
- Give as a form of sacrifice to God (Philippians 4:18).
- Give as an acknowledgment of one's stewardship before God in this life (1 Corinthians 6:19b-20a).
- Give as part of one's accountability to God (Romans 14:10-12).
- Give as a concrete proof of love (2 Corinthians 8:8, 24).
- Give the self before any material gift (2 Corinthians 8:5).
- Give voluntarily (2 Corinthians 8:3; 9:5; 9:7).
- Give proportionately as God prospers (1 Corinthians 16:2; 2 Corinthians 8:12).
- Give generously (2 Corinthians 8:2; 9:11).
- Give systematically (1 Corinthians 16:2).
- Give in love (1 Corinthians 13:3).
- Give as an expression of your faith (2 Corinthians 9:13).
- Give cheerfully/gladly (2 Corinthians 9:7).
- Give as an expression of trust, privilege, and responsibility (1 Corinthians 4:11-15).
- Give in response to God the creator, owner, redeemer, and sustainer (Colossians 1:15-21).
- Give to please God (Philippians 4:18).
- Give in response to the resurrection (1 Corinthians 15:1-58; 16:1-4).

The Pastor Affirms Stewardship

The teaching of stewardship principles is a primary task of the pulpit. Failing to talk about stewardship is as much a dereliction of duty as failing to talk about the cross of Christ. For the cross is the highest expression of stewardship. Our Lord wrote the ultimate stewardship message with his very life. And if we believe the message of the cross we must be equally concerned about the mission of the cross which channels itself through the church. We are stewards of the message and the pledging, giving, and use of money is a vital and necessary part of that witness. Stewardship is a spiritual force that performs miracles with money given in response to the Great Commission.

II. Trainer Advocate
Training The Governing Board Of The Local Church

Every governing board should engage in a serious study of stewardship. Such a study will further equip the governing body in fulfilling the responsibility of challenging the people of God with the privilege of responsible Christian stewardship of money, time, and talents.

In addition, members of the governing body can be challenged to grapple with the full meaning of stewardship as it pertains to all of life. And they should be challenged to address the stewardship of money in their own lives as they set an example and seek to encourage the stewardship and mission understanding of their particular congregation.

Each governing board should develop its own philosophy of stewardship. Such a statement can affirm biblical concepts of stewardship, suggest a program of individual and corporate growth, and point a congregation toward long-range possibilities. It could contain mission goals and offer new levels of growth-in-giving. This resource, developed by the governing body with input from the congregation, is invaluable for training new members and communicants. (See page 49.)

Advocate

The pastor serves as a mission advocate with the governing body. This means continually challenging the governing body to enlarge the sphere of mission consciousness and increase mission giving. It means regularly reviewing the benevolence portion of the total church budget and developing goals for increasing proportionate responsibility. A congregation can be stimulated by new and exciting visions of expanding and enriching mission service opportunities.

The pastor serves as an advocate for stewardship by analyzing with the governing body the potential of the congregation. Are we living up to our potential as a unit of mission? The effectiveness of any church will be measured in part, at least, by its faithfulness in training, encouraging, and challenging its members in responsible financial stewardship that leads to increased mission involvement.

The pastor is an advocate for personal stewardship commitment on the part of the church officers. In many congregations the officers and pastoral staff make their pledges in advance of Stewardship Sunday. The weekly or annual amount, without names, or the total amount and number of contributors is then published in the church newsletter or bulletin. This type of leadership example shows the congregation that the pastor(s) and officers are themselves persuaded by the gospel and the evidence of human need in the world to do generous, proportionate, and disciplined giving. The congregation can be taught and encouraged in responsible stewardship by the leadership example and obvious commitment of the officers and pastor(s). This form of witness needs no apology.

III. Enabler/Counselor

"The professional leader also carries a stewardship responsibility as an enabler within the congregation. Ephesians 4:11 describes that task as one of equipping the saints for the work of the ministry." (Richard B. Cunningham, *Creative Stewardship*, Nashville, Abingdon, 1979, p. 116)

The pastor as enabler may counsel with the session to appoint a committee or assign an existing one the responsibility for developing a brochure describing for the congregation its total mission involvement. No person is fully aware of what one's particular church is doing or its many relationships. Highlight specific projects of the local congregation. Describe the congregation's partnership in mission and what it helps to do through other governing bodies of the particular denomination and in ecumenical relationships.

Some serious thought and creative imagination can result in a brochure which shows how the particular congregation is involved in a multitude of activities directly or indirectly. Informed members respond through increased gifts. Such an interpretive piece can be used as a basic reference at stewardship visitation time. Use it as well to inform community newcomers and new members about what the particular church is doing in the world. This affirmation points to the place of Christian stewardship and the importance of mission to the congregation as well as to those who might be considering membership.

Counselor

The pastor has many opportunities for encouraging members to consider Christian stewardship in making a will. This can be done in various ways. Information can be disseminated at the initiative of the pastor or a Wills Emphasis Committee regarding the use of accumulated resources for mission. It can be mentioned in sermons and included in bulletin announcements or the church newsletter. When bequests are received by the church it is appropriate to include the name of the donor in the bulletin, the designation of the bequest, and appropriate words of thanks and encouragement to consider such an example.

Trust relationships develop through pastoral care and leadership. Parishioners from time to time wish to discuss matters relating to making or revising a will. They may seek counsel on projects in the life of the congregation or denomination that could benefit from financial support. Candor and direct responses are appreciated by those who request such information, and positive interpretation opens doors of infinite possibility. In such counseling the perceptive pastor may find opportunity for encouraging individuals to enhance a self-centered lifestyle that needs to reach out in love to others for Christ's sake.

On occasions, the pastor may feel moved to take the initiative and make a personal visit for the purpose of suggesting a will that includes the local church and/or the church-at-large. This is not taking advantage of a trust, as some might rationalize, but affirming a positive stewardship witness which enables individuals to grow in Christian commitment and grateful acknowledgment of God's redeeming love. Enabling others in their stewardship growth and Christian witness is not to be considered as manipulation. Rather, it is a natural response out of one's own commitment to use every opportunity in cultivating the stewardship of others.

IV. Manager/Administrator

"... the minister cannot evade the role of the chief administrator of his/her church, related to every aspect of the congregational life. The administrator is 'the manager' — one who is capable of organizing and executing a program." (L. R. Ditzen, *The Minister's Desk Book*, West Nyack, Parker Publishing, 1968, p. 1)

The minister assists in planning, organizing, implementing, and measuring the various stewardship and mission projects in the local church, but does not do it alone. The minister

- connects people whose projects would benefit from working together;
- disseminates material, information, resources to appropriate committees or individuals within the church network;
- helps recruit stewardship and mission committee members;
- assists in stewardship promotion and publicity;
- encourages the stewardship committee through participation in its meetings;
- serves as a resource person in stewardship strategy planning;
- promotes sound management practices as part of the stewardship of local church operations;
- and above all, preaches positive stewardship sermons.

The pastor usually receives all denominational information and communications regarding stewardship and mission and special offerings. As administrator the pastor is responsible for channeling such information to appropriate chairpersons or staff members for maximum use of such material. Whoever prepares the weekly bulletin or monthly newsletter or stewardship publicity needs to receive whatever will be most helpful to keep the congregation informed about mission.

From time to time appropriate suggestions can be added about how or when such information might appear. Often issues of concern need to be addressed or emphasized because of a particular committee reaction or publication. Managing the flow of information, highlighting it from specialized insights, and following up on use and application reflects good stewardship in the administration of stewardship.

Careful oversight and reminders of good office practices and building use are other obvious messages of stewardship practices. Simple and sound practices of economy can show a marked savings in the total church budget. Such messages are not lost on the congregation.

V. Personal Example And Lifestyle

"There is one other element, not previously listed, which may be of as much importance, or more, as we consider the pastor's role. It has to do with the pastor as steward. Members of the congregation have a sixth sense about this. They seem to know whether the pastor is 'all talk' or is in fact striving with them to achieve good personal stewardship habits. Dr. Hermann in his book, *The Chief Steward*, maintains that the example of the pastor in giving, prayer, Bible study, and the use of time and money is the key to effective stewardship in the congregation." (Mark Landfried, *This Service of Love*, Pennsylvania, The Synod of the Trinity, 1978, p. 57)

Giving is for everyone and the pastor leads the way. The pastor can never ask of the congregation what she or he is not also doing personally. Paul says to Timothy, "... set the believers an example ..." (1 Timothy 4:12). The Chairman of the Stewardship Committee gets a message if the pastor's pledge comes drifting in after the suggested deadline for the congregation, or never arrives. The Treasurer gets a message if the pastor gives irregularly, doesn't increase the pledge after asking others to do so, or seldom fulfills the pledge.

By the same token a pastor who tithes or gives above the tithe should make no apology for testifying to that fact when the official board discusses stewardship or from the pulpit when giving personal witness to the meaning of stewardship or with a member who comes for counsel regarding proportionate giving. In preaching, a simple "one-liner" at the conclusion of a sermon on tithing or "stepping up" can sincerely indicate that the pastor would never ask of others what was not already being personally practiced. That kind of affirmation is respected and noted by the congregation.

Sound management of one's economic resources is a characteristic of an informed Christian lifestyle. Discretion in money matters and a high standard of responsibility leaves a positive message to which no one can take exception when the pulpit speaks of accountability.

What about accountability with time and talent? Good work habits and a program of skill development are part of the discipline of vocational stewardship. Dr. James Glasse in his book, *Putting it Together in the Parish*, says that the pastor must "pay the rent" required by the parish that supports his or her ministry. This is the responsibility of the pastor. The primary commitment of the pastor's time and talent is to the parish served and not the other way around. "Paying the rent" with time and talent sends a positive subliminal stewardship message to the congregation. Glasse ends the chapter on "Paying the Rent" by saying: "Blessed is that pastor who has paid the rent; she/he has time (and talent) to give to other pursuits."

Conclusion

Christian stewardship is discipleship that calls forth a faithful and fitting response to God's grace. The pastor has a vital role in cultivating the grace of stewardship in the life of individual parishioners and the corporate life of the congregation. Christ, God's Chief Steward, is our model. Through our practice and preaching of stewardship we reaffirm our partnership, and that of our parishioners, in the message of the cross with him who personally wrote that message with his very life. Stewardship is at the heart of discipleship. In the words of Wallace Fischer: "Jesus' stewardship of God's mysteries is the living model for his fellows. Stewardship is every Christian's true vocation. Stewardship is every congregation's primary responsibility."

The Local Church As A Stewardship Model

Introduction

"After ten years as a pastor, I have discovered a simple, almost obvious, truth about stewardship. The truth is that one of the best ways people in our congregation learn about stewardship is by watching how we as pastors and elders choose to spend the church's resources. For instance, if we as a session (governing body) choose to spend very little of our congregation's resources on people and ministries outside of ourselves, by example we teach members to take care of themselves first and give only what is left over to God.

"The opposite is true too. When a church is generous in its giving to mission outside of itself, when it sacrifices luxuries, frills, sometimes even necessities to see that Christ's words and works of love are shared with others, then that church teaches its members to be generous too.

"When a church pledges a significant percent of its budget to mission, it teaches its members to think percentages rather than amounts when giving to the church and encourages growth in proportionate giving.

"The way we as pastors and elders budget our congregation's resources teaches our members how to budget their resources. Ralph Waldo Emerson once observed, 'All children have at least one thing in common. They close their ears to advice but open their eyes to example.' When it comes to stewardship, I think there are a lot of wide open eyes out there in our congregations." (Mike Pulsifer, *Stewardship by Example*, published in *Monday Morning*, April 4, 1977. Used by permission)

Responsibility For Congregational Proportionate Giving

"The being of stewards is not only the vocation of individual Christians, it is the mission of the whole church. I want to accentuate the verb: stewardship *is* the church's mission. Rightly to understand the depths of this old/new symbol of the Christian life is to know that the mission of the church *is* its stewardship." (Douglas John Hall, *The Steward: A Biblical Symbol Come of Age*, New York, Friendship Press, 1982, p. 130)

The corporate faith of a congregation is demonstrated by what a church does with its money even as an individual's giving should be an indication of the reality of that person's faith: "... your very giving proves the reality of your faith" (2 Corinthians 9:13 J. B. Phillips). By the same token an individual is strengthened in his/her convictions, and corresponding tangible response, by the attitude, philosophy, and example of his/her particular church. The church is accountable before God for its faithfulness to its own calling as a witnessing community with worldwide involvement.

"Just as the individual's stewardship of material resources reflects his values and ordering of life so does the church's use of its material resources reflect its priorities and spiritual health." (Richard B. Cunningham, *Creative Stewardship*, Nashville, Tennessee, Abingdon, 1979, p. 118)

The pastor is responsible for the spiritual life of the congregation. A vital component of spiritual health is financial health. The pastor has an essential role along with the official board(s) of the congregation in the responsibility and obligation for maintaining and enlarging a responsible proportionate benevolence budget. This includes: increasing the benevolence percentage each year, honoring benevolence commitments in the same way all other commitments are honored, including a benevolence proportion in congregational capital fund endeavors, and establishing a policy which indicates that a portion of all undesignated special gifts will be used for benevolent purposes.

The Church And Its Mission

"How much will we give to others and what will we spend on ourselves?" is the basic and fundamental question every church official board needs to ask itself. When a church asks itself that question and attempts to answer it with an honest and earnest proportionate budget, then and only then does it have the right to ask its individual members the same question. Asking for proportionate sacrificial commitment on the part of the congregation places a similar commitment on the official board. The mission we preach is the mission that we must practice. And that begins in the local church as a responsibility of its official board: in planning, budgeting, practice, and payment.

When the church loses its sense of mission it loses its reason for being. Karl Barth once remarked that the greatest peril facing the church is "its own churchiness," meaning the church's passion to perpetuate its own institutional forms at the expense of its saving mission in the world. Dr. Wallace Fisher puts it more bluntly: "Biblical stewardship is a lifestyle with the Cross at the center. The church must challenge, inform, and persuade its community to embody God's Word in the world if it expects to be a force in society rather than a fungus on it." (Wallace E. Fisher, *A New Climate for Stewardship*, Nashville, Abingdon, 1976, p. 15)

To become self-centered, either purposely or carelessly, is to betray a sacred trust and erode the true meaning of stewardship which is worldwide in scope. No congregation contains or represents the whole mission of the whole church. In the late 1960s and early 1970s the then United Presbyterian Church was in a mission funding crisis. Although total giving was increasing, receipts for approved governing body mission (Presbytery, Synod, and General Assembly) actually decreased. Individual churches were increasingly looking after their own needs, in some cases spending lavishly on themselves while growing increasingly myopic about mission. In short, the church was turning inward rather than going into all the world.

A ground swell of Presbyterian concern about this urgent problem found expression in the 184th (1974) General Assembly's overwhelming vote to put in place a new mission support program which would challenge the denomination to increase mission giving dramatically in the years ahead. A conscious decision was made to address the matter creatively. A new emphasis was placed on financial health and wholeness and year-round stewardship education enabling people to grow toward their potential as stewards of God's purpose in history and enabling congregations to grow toward their potential as communities of faithful stewards.

Fulfilling Our Potential

Are we living up to our potential as a unit of mission? Unfulfilled potential is possibly withheld. The effectiveness of any church will be measured in part, at least, by its faithfulness in training and encouraging its members in responsible stewardship. This includes the challenge of an accountable Christian lifestyle and nurture in the discipline of discipleship. Financial stewardship serves as a barometer of faithfulness to God's purpose and financial health is a matter of the spiritual health of congregations.

When the church talks about money, it needs to understand itself as inviting people to express their faith through tangible means. We give to God through a budget that is not an end but a means. With that understanding, the whole stewardship process is changed. We no longer buy something or pay for something. Rather we affirm something that cannot be measured. We respond in love to God's love revealed in Jesus Christ our Lord and Savior. "The church cannot be a good steward of its material resources without urging generous, joyful, and sacrificial giving to the church. And because of the importance of giving, the church should not be hesitant, embarrassed, or apologetic in doing so." (Richard B. Cunningham, *Creative Stewardship*, Nashville, Abingdon, 1979, p. 119)

Stewardship growth and accountability means recognizing and living up to our potential. The official board(s) needs to test itself from time to time by asking some practical and realistic questions. What are our stewardship capabilities and how are we measuring up? What is the median income of our community? Does our per capita giving reflect a reasonable percentage of that potential? How does our per capita giving compare with the entire denomination or churches of comparable size in our presbytery (area grouping of churches in our denomination)?

The local church is a stewardship model. What it does with its responsibility has worldwide implications. The church is in mission because Christ has called it to be in mission. It is in mission through the various governing bodies of our many denominations. It is in mission locally, regionally, nationally, and around the world. The church is concerned with funding because money is essential for doing Christ's mission. In the words of Dr. Harry Emerson

Fosdick: "The avenues are open down which our pennies, our dollars, or our millions can walk together in an accumulating multitude to the succor of all humanity."

While the church is in mission through its various governing bodies, the responsibility for the funding of mission focuses on the local congregation and its growth potential through the leadership of the pastor and official board(s). "Much is required from the person (church) to whom much is given; and more is required from the person (church) to whom much more is given" (Luke 12:48b GNB).

Part II

New Member Training

Part II

The Disciple As A Steward

A Statement On Christian Stewardship

Christian stewardship is discipleship and, as such, it calls us to manage and use resources — both *spiritual and material* — in a faithful and fitting response to God. It has to do with the priorities and styles of our lives — our consumption of the earth's resources, the care of our bodies, the cultivation of our minds, our use of time for ourselves and others, the sharing of our skills and abilities, and the spending and giving of our money. In every resource, the Christian steward sees responsibility as an occasion for gratitude, and the opportunity to serve God, oneself, and one's neighbor in love.

We bring nothing into this world and take nothing out of it. Everything that we have while we are here comes as a gift from God. In appreciation, we choose to share a portion of these gifts through our stewardship of *time, talent, and treasure*. We must budget our hours so that we are able to give time to fulfill God's plan. God gives everyone potential talents when we are born so that we can share in God's plan in our own unique way. The stewardship of our treasure is an ongoing process of regular and systematic giving.

Our church believes that we can best achieve the faithful stewardship God calls us to by applying the principle of **Proportionate Giving**. A **Proportionate Giver** is one who covenants with God to give to the work of the church a set proportion of all received from God. This portion is seen as God's and is given first from all that comes to us. By study of God's Word, and by daily life with the Risen Lord, we keep our hearts open to increasing this proportion as Christ leads us to deeper understanding and further commitments. We believe, therefore, in giving careful consideration to becoming percentage givers in order that we may have a specific starting point on a road which encompasses the doctrine of tithing and moves beyond it to the total surrender of all that we have and all that we are. Based on this approach, our church says to each member, "We are not concerned with your share of our church budget. What really matters is God's share of your life — time, talent, and treasure."

Our church believes that this principle, **Proportionate Giving**, must also apply to the church and the gifts it receives in response to God from members. In keeping with this, Westminster Church pledges a first portion of congregational receipts to benevolence causes and to the work of the kingdom beyond our own doors, and is further committed to faithful growth in this proportion.

Our whole life is a partnership with God. We cannot "give anything to God; but we can know the joy of serving God by using God's gifts wisely and sharing them with others. Each of us can live as God's steward." (From *New Members Training Manual*, Westminster Presbyterian Church of Grand Rapids, Michigan. Used with permission)

Mission And Stewardship: Fulfilling The Mandate

A Training Session For New Members

The church of Jesus Christ is not a religious club; it is a witnessing society. Our Lord still speaks to us today as he spoke to his disciples in that resurrection appearance saying: "... you will be my witnesses in Jerusalem, in all Judea and Samaria, and to the ends of the earth" (Acts 1:8b NRSV). Our Lord wasn't offering options, he was mandating mission.

As Christians we have been called and committed to be at work in the world. We are partners in ministry and mission throughout the earth. We are involved in tearing down walls of separation and in building bridges of reconciliation. We have been given a mission, a commission, and a relationship with God through Jesus Christ. We are under command and obligation.

In jungle, swamp, and desert — on mountain height and frozen waste — in haunts of wretchedness and despair — by lonely river and dark forest — in asphalt jungle, through remote prairie, on to dusty reservations and barren tundra, the message goes out. The witness goes on — preaching good news to the poor — release to the captives of mental and spiritual tyranny — healing for the helpless — sight to the imperceptive — liberty to those burdened with sin and guilt — hope to those in despair.

This is our witness for we are called to be disciples "... to the ends of the earth," he said — beginning at home and moving concentrically outward. In education, evangelism, agriculture, vocational training, social redirection and redevelopment — the message of Christ becomes a leavening influence — personal and social. The gospel of love revealed in Jesus Christ is the good news of salvation from sin, holistic hope, and the promotion of social righteousness.

In local church, in regional and international governing bodies, his redemptive purposes are at work and we are partners in it

— part of the endless line of splendor — keeping faith with his commands and commitment — enlarging the transforming power of the cross. In new church development — in refugee camps — feeding the hungry — in centers of transition — in youth camps and conferences and in seminaries and colleges, the Spirit is at work.

In retreats and training events — in orphanages and homes for the infirm — in daycare centers and literacy clinics — in emergency relief, hunger programs, and peacemaking projects — in sanctuaries for the wayward, the backward, the downtrodden, and the beaten up, the Spirit of the Lord is there and we are there — because we are called to be, challenged to be, and mandated to be.

Look again at the imperative which our Lord first delivered to his disciples, but to us as well, when he said: "... (go) to the ends of the earth." When the mandate was given, our Lord was speaking to eleven people. They had no idea of the immensity of the task. But they had no doubt about its urgency. They were given a responsibility for the local church: Jerusalem. Yes, the local church must become the home base, the source of strength, the foundation stone of the larger structure. And some may say, "We have so much going on in the local church, is it necessary to do more?" But no church is merely local. Our Lord commanded us to go beyond ourselves. It is not a matter of choice. It is a mandate.

The local church is only the beginning! Judea was the next larger region. So the local church is commanded to move beyond its immediate commitments to the larger area which is served by a regional governing body. Samaria was beyond that — an area in the present we might define as a grouping of governing bodies in this country to form a national arena. And to the ends of the earth is just what it says — everywhere. This is addressed by the world mission enterprise of the various denominations. (The three areas can be defined more specifically by a particular denominational definition and the description of the mission and services provided can be interpreted.)

Our Lord was very explicit. To him it was not a question of either/or. It was a matter of all and everywhere. Minister at home. Minister in regional areas. Minister in the national arena. Minister throughout the world — "to the ends of the earth." The mandate is the same in its urgency. That is the answer to the question so often raised about the number of needs at home without going elsewhere. The imperative is not for us to speculate about but to fulfill! We are what God is doing in the world today at home and abroad.

Money is part of that mission. Apart from the church's ministry through people and their gifts, God has no other plan for the world's salvation. Stewardship is a vital component and essential ingredient in mission. Biblical stewardship is a lifestyle with a cross at the center. It is every congregation's primary responsibility. As John Douglas Hall says, "The being of stewards is not only the vocation of individual Christians, it is the mission of the whole church."

When we give to the church we are not paying dues nor are we paying pew rent. We are fulfilling our vows of church membership. When one joins the church and makes a profession of faith in Jesus Christ as Lord and Savior, implicit in those vows is the commitment to participate in the life and work of Christ's church through the use of our time, talent, and treasure. It is reputed that Martin Luther once said there are two kinds of conversion — the conversion of the heart and the conversion of the pocketbook. Many pastors would agree that the conversion of the heart seems to come more easily than the conversion of the pocketbook. In actuality our financial support of the church is sacramental in nature. And we need to see it that way. A sacrament is an outward act with an inner meaning — a visible sign of an invisible grace.

Giving to the cause of Christ through the church is an opportunity and a privilege, not a legalistic obligation nor onerous duty. In Old Testament days a good Jew was obligated to keep over 600 laws which placed requirements on every aspect of living. Our Lord changed that with the word "love," when he summarized the Law: "You shall love the Lord your God with all your heart, and with all your soul, and with all your strength, and with all your mind; and your neighbor as yourself" (Luke 10:27). This summarizes the Ten Commandments in which the first four deal with one's relationship to God and the last six deal with one's relationship to one's neighbor.

Religion is both spiritual and practical. The spiritual is vertical in which one seeks to be in a relationship with God: the totality of you loving God. The practical is horizontal, loving your neighbor as yourself. This means reaching out to the world in love. It takes the form of a cross. And in taking the form of a cross we are informed by the cross. We seek to do God's will and we seek to share Christ's love. Faith and action. And that is what stewardship is: our faith in action, imprinted by the cross.

The offering on Sunday morning is not merely a routine event in which we camouflage the paying of the rent by sweet sounds of organic melody or a well-rendered anthem by the choir. The offering is an act of worship, an affirmation of highest praise, and an expression of deepest devotion. It is celebrative in nature as a time of thanksgiving and praise. It is sacramental in nature and needs to be seen and understood in that way. A sacrament is an outward and visible act with an inner and spiritual meaning.

The offering follows the sermon as the people's response to the word of God. It is also the congregation's fullest participation in the service of worship. And as the offering is being received, in the mind's eye, the walls of the sanctuary must move aside and the worshiper needs to catch a vision of the whole world to which we as Christians are called to minister in the name of Jesus Christ. Through the offering, we move outside of ourselves and beyond ourselves in broader service following the Great Commission of our Lord to go out into all the world baptizing and teaching in his name (Matthew 28:19-20). Through our expressions of love and devotion, given with prayers of gratitude for all God's mercies, we also help to carry out our Lord's Great Commission.

We invite every member of this church to make a pledge. Next week you will receive in the mail your offering envelopes and a pledge card. We invite every member to make a pledge and to renew that pledge annually. All pledges are held in strictest confidence. However, a pledge may be adjusted at any time by calling the Financial Secretary. No questions are asked and no comments made. There are times when circumstances change and a pledge must be adjusted. Make no apology; we understand. By the same token there are times when one may receive an unexpected increase in income. By all means, feel free to call and adjust your pledge upward.

This church and its mission depend on the giving of the members of the congregation. We are not a wealthy church. Some people think we are, but we are not. We do have a modest endowment fund. However, all income received from the endowment fund is designated (for mission, for capital improvements, and so on). If the church has a substantial endowment fund, this is the place to indicate what the designations are for and a rationale for needing the support of every member of the congregation in regard to the operating fund. Each quarter you will receive a statement. It is not really a statement, however, but an indication of where you are in your giving. It may help jog your memory. At the same time, it will carry a message from the Board of Trustees telling what is being accomplished by your gifts and those of other members of the congregation. There may be a message from one of our missionaries or a thank you note from one of the ministries in our community that you help to support. We want you to have a sense of partnership in all that your church is doing.

We invite you to read again *Our Philosophy Of Stewardship* which is contained in your membership packet. There is also a time and talent sheet that you may fill out. We are stewards of our time and talents as well as our treasure. There are many places in the life of this congregation where you can help make a difference. We urge you to find a place, or places, where you can use your skills and give of your time and energy.

A Time For Reflection

Some Thoughts On Making A Church Pledge

We do not give to God by meeting a budget. Stewardship is too often thought of in terms of budgets, formulas, or goals to be met. Dollar amounts can illustrate and help interpret directions, needs, and dreams, but without a sound theological basis they can be enervating and elicit only a mechanical response.

We do not give to God by meeting a budget. We give to God through a budget which is not an end, but a means. With this understanding the whole stewardship process is changed. We are no longer paying for something; rather we are affirming something. We are responding in love to God's love revealed in Christ. With this kind of insight, figures become minimal guidelines for open-end, unlimited, sacrificial sharing. Making a pledge is a spiritual experience. *And it is a time for reflection!*

One of the things I still reflect on during the stewardship season is a scene from my childhood. Every Saturday evening my father would seat himself at the dining room table and take from his pocket an envelope with his earnings for the week. It was a solemn occasion.

Those were the "Great Depression" years when even copper coins were terribly precious. My father labored long and lovingly for the contents of that little envelope. It represented some sixty hours of hard work at his little store, and additional hours of record keeping and letter writing at home. Reaching inside, he withdrew the contents — $33 in one dollar bills and coins. A modest yet adequate amount for those traumatic times. And while I gazed in awe another drama took place before my very eyes. Very carefully my father first took $3.33 and placed that amount in an envelope marked "Church." That money was his tithe, and it was sacred. It was never touched except to be presented in the house of the Lord on the first day of the week. It always came off the top. Everything else was secondary.

Then following the ritual of placing coins and bills in other envelopes — for mortgage payments, food, clothing, and other necessities of life. At times it was a long and painful process. Often a purchase or payment needed to be postponed until a later date. So be it. But there was never any question about what was first and foremost. Saturday night was a time for reflection. It was a time to reaffirm his values and exercise his priorities. This was a sacred moment, as sacred as the highest act of worship. For this was worship of the highest order: "What shall I return to the Lord for all his bounty to me?" (Psalm 116:12 NRSV).

We also need to reflect on the fact that there is a definite relationship between money and religion. We cannot separate the two, much as we try at times. The teaching of stewardship principles is a primary task and responsibility of the church. A church that fails to talk about stewardship is as guilty of dereliction of duty as the church that fails to talk about the cross of Christ during Holy Week.

The cross is the highest expression of stewardship. And if we believe the message of the cross, we must be concerned about the mission of the cross — the mission that is channeled through the church. We are stewards of that message and that mission. We have been bought with a price. We have been bought for a purpose. What we are and do as Christians has a theological foundation.

Being a steward is a faith response to the grace of God revealed in Jesus Christ our Lord. The pledging and giving of money for Christ and his church is a personal act of gratitude, an expression of witness, and an affirmation of discipleship. Our membership vows include a confession of faith in Jesus Christ as Lord and Savior. They also include a commitment to stewardship and service, ministry and mission, work and witness. Wallace Fisher says, "Stewardship is every Christian's true vocation. It is every congregation's primary responsibility."

"A person may decide either to accept or reject Jesus Christ," Luther Powell writes in *Money and the Church*, "but once he/she has accepted Christ, it is not for that person to decide whether or not to be a steward, for one becomes a steward when one becomes a Christian ... That person has been entrusted with the gospel of Jesus Christ and has been given the gift of eternal life, and it is one's high calling to share this gift with others. The only requirement that is placed on a steward is that the person be found faithful." (Luther Powell, *Money and the Church*, New York, Association Press, 1962, p. 236)

As we reflect, we need to reaffirm our call to mission, which is actually Christ's mandate. It is not an option. It is a command: "... you will be my witness in Jerusalem, in all Judea and Samaria and to the ends of the earth" (Acts 1:8 NRSV). Our Lord was very explicit. We have a commitment to the church where we belong (our "Jerusalem") because it is a ministry and mission center. We also have a commitment to minister in the larger community and throughout the world. The mandate is not for us to speculate about, but to fulfill. We are what God is doing in the world today, at home and abroad.

And money is a vital part of mission. Apart from the church's ministry through people and their gifts, God has no other plan for the world's salvation. Stewardship and mission are inseparable. Taking time to reflect prepares one to make a faith pledge, rather than perform a reflex response, that truly glorifies God and reaches out in ministry and mission to others. As Christians, we have been called to, and voluntarily accept, an awesome responsibility. When we make our pledge and present our gifts to substantiate our pledge, we are literally making a profession of faith. As Saint Paul says, "... your very giving proves the reality of your faith" (2 Corinthians 9:13 J. B. Phillips).

Those things to which we truly commit ourselves become costly enterprises. But when commitments are being fulfilled, when promises are being kept, when deeds are being done, discipleship expressed and love manifested in the name of Christ, then there is the joy of celebration. For we are sharing the good news out of which comes our own spiritual renewal and the joy of genuine self-giving which God experiences in every moment of the universe's existence.

We reach out in the name of Christ because we are called to be his disciples and "... stewards of the manifold grace of God ..." (1 Peter 4:10a NRSV). Such a high calling requires times of reflection to enlarge and enhance our pilgrimage of faith and works. (Allan J. Weenink, *Presbyterian Survey*, October, 1992. Used with permission)

Our Philosophy Of Financial Support

Christ Church Of Main Street

When you promise financial support to Christ Church:

1. You are accepting Christ's call to be involved responsibly, by supporting the work of the church through the giving of money, time, and talent.

2. The pledge card you will receive after you join the church is a record of your intended investment. It is a voluntary statement of your commitment upon which your church bases its expenditures, makes its plans, and carries forward its total program.

3. Your "investment" may be raised or lowered as your financial circumstances change significantly. One needs only to call the church office and adjustments will be made in a courteous and confidential manner. Each year you will be asked to rethink your financial commitment and to make a new pledge. This encourages a process of spiritual growth through stewardship.

4. You will be participating in a truly Christian plan of financial giving. This is called **Proportionate Giving**. All gifts are given in proportion to one's worldly means: "... in proportion as the Lord may prosper you." The Bible says that we should give ten percent of our income. That ten percent includes *all* charitable giving. If you can't begin with ten percent then start with a smaller proportion and increase when you are able.

5. The Church of Jesus Christ is a significant enterprise. What the church does, its members make possible through their prayers, service, and tangible support of the program. The vast and far-flung areas of spiritual concern at home and abroad are maintained by the sacrificial sharing of those who are deeply concerned, committed Christians. If we don't do it, who else will?

6. You will be given offering envelopes, for they make all gifts equal in the sight of persons. All pledges are held in strict confidence.

7. The church budget is developed in communities that are chaired by Elders and resourced by the staff. It is reviewed by the Stewardship Committee and Trustees before it is submitted to the Session for approval. The congregation is asked to endorse the budget at the January Annual Meeting following the fall Stewardship Campaign.

8. You are assured of a policy of limited special offerings, which must first be approved by the Session.

9. In considering a total pledge to the church, one should keep in mind that children and youth are invited to contribute to the General Budget using their own pledge cards and offering envelopes as a method of developing good stewardship habits while in church school. Also, our Association of Church Women does not engage in fund-raising activities such as bazaars, carnivals, or bake sales. The Association is supported by the pledges of members. Therefore, when making a pledge to the church, take into consideration the above factors.

10. You will receive a financial receipt every three months indicating the church's record of your giving. This is not a "bill." Rather, it is an accounting for your personal files. It also indicates the accuracy of church records and perhaps at times, may be a friendly reminder.

The Church of Jesus Christ depends on dedicated, realistic, sacrificial, and loving stewardship!

My Pledge

MY pledge is an expression of my loyalty to my church.

MY pledge is an open confession that I believe in orderly methods of sharing in the mission of my church and do so with integrity.

MY pledge is a revelation of my faith in the gospel of Christ.

MY pledge is my response to the call in the world around me for love, light, peace, and hope.

MY pledge, together with those of my fellow members, reveals the moral strength and spiritual awareness of my church.

MY pledge represents the value and worth which I attach to my religion.

MY pledge is a sacred covenant of responsible involvement.

MY pledge is a joyous affirmation of my call to discipleship.

Pledging

The discipline of making a financial commitment to support mission through the work of your congregation helps to strength faith. It is a reminder of your relationships within the community of believers, relationships which connect you with others the world over who proclaim the lordship of Christ. The personal value of seriously considering your financial commitment and making a pledge to Christ's Church requires taking time to discover the place where you put your faith, hope, and trust. (From the pamphlet *Pledging* produced by the Presbyterian Church U.S.A. #918-01-119)

Part III

Stewardship Sermons

Neither Poverty Nor Riches

Matthew 19; Proverbs 30

Linda A. Knieriemen

Money advertises. That's right, besides its obvious use as the vehicle of exchange, money functions as a political and religious commercial. Since antiquity, symbols and mottos printed on coins and now bills have circulated a message from the leaders to the population.

In Rome, in the first century, Augustus produced coins showing himself as the "son of the divine Caesar" on one side, with the stamp of the goddess, Peace, standing on the reverse. Even the illiterate understood that Augustus was to be considered as the son of a god and the bringer of peace. In Palestine, Pontius Pilate chose to place on his bronze coins an image of the ladle used to pour libations to the pagan gods on one side and the curved staff borne by Roman priests on the other.

In the United States, our coins and our bills all read boldly, *In God We Trust.* The commercial tells the world what we want them to believe about us as a nation. *In God We Trust.* First used on coins printed in 1864, it became the motto of the United States and assumed its place on all our coins and bills.

But, in this most materialistic nation of the world, this motto seems puzzling. Is it still true or is it a case of false advertising? Has it simply become something we ignore and don't even think about? When Baby Boomers, fearing the end of Social Security, worry over the status of their portfolios and seeing the value of their stocks soar more than they play with their kids, and at the same time stop attending church and synagogue, I'm not sure we can claim this motto as descriptive of our church, and maybe even of our society. As a society, and as religious people in particular, do we even intend to trust in God? Can you say it is true for you? Do you trust in God more than you trust in what those words are printed on?

The question of where we place our trust, and more specifically, what we believe God would have us do and believe relative to money, are not new questions. A Rich Young Man, possibly in his twenties, a good citizen, a good Jew, posed such a question to Jesus: "Is it enough to obey the commandments?" "No," Jesus said, "you must trust God with all of your life, including your finances. Your attachment to property has its bondage. Give your 'stuff' away to the poor. Otherwise, your treasure will not be in God's Realm where you claim you want to spend eternity." Religiosity, piety, and mottos on coins became laughable and condemn us if we don't put our actions where our advertising is.

Early saints, from Augustine to Ambrose to Chrysostom to Clement, addressed this issue in their time. John Calvin offers his opinion to the sixteenth century elite in Geneva when he says in a small work, *De Luxo* — "On Luxury" — "We are worse than children delighting in cheap necklaces. We (the Reformers) wish people would follow a moderation closer to abstinence than to luxury."

This morning's sermon could have served as a preface to this Stewardship Season, but instead it will serve as a postscript. This morning we will take a brief look at what the Bible has to say about faith and wealth. The laws of Moses, the prophets, the wisdom literature, and Jesus, all speak to this issue. In fact, Jesus talks as much or more about the perils of wealth as he does any other subject. We find in scripture diverse statements about money.

God says to Abraham, "I will give to you a land flowing with milk and honey." (God sends material blessings.)

And **Amos**, who scolds the greedy women in Samaria, "You cows of Bashan (and where there are cows there are bulls, so this means everyone) who oppress the poor and crush the needy. The time is coming when they shall take you away with hooks." Alluding to the Babylonian exile. (Undistributed wealth will be punished.)

Jesus says, "You will have the poor with you always," (often misinterpreted as "You don't need to worry about them") and "It is harder for a camel to go through the eye of the needle than for a rich person to get into heaven." (The rich are not godly.)

Theologies surrounding money are many and sometimes they directly oppose each other. As we look at a few, I invite you to think about what motto or symbol illustrates your relationship with money. What would you engrave on your own coins?

I'll get started: Based on their reading of select verses of scripture some would adopt "Wealth Is Evil" as a motto on their currency, illustrated by a symbol of a pile of bills with a heavy slash through it.

Is wealth (defined as undistributed riches and surplus possession) inherently evil? Writer Ron Sider in his book, *Rich Christians in an Age of Hunger*, and Jim Wallis in his highly respected and widely circulated *Sojourners* magazine might like to see this motto on coins in their pockets. Informed by the words of prophets like Amos, Jesus' parables, and the Sermon on the Mount, they claim that wealth is sinful especially in the face of our global economy where the rich are still getting richer and using more resources and the poor are still getting poorer.

God, they say, stands with the poor, making our task as rich Christians (and by their definition, nearly all Americans, and America as a society as well) responsible for the promotion of justice and dignity for all people. Christians must demonstrate this in their individual lifestyle, and as a people, by confronting systemic evil. By redistributing our wealth these writers say we are able to stand with God on the side of the poor. Probably many of us should consider just such a discipline.

It has been for me a compelling and radical position, standing in stark contrast to our materialistically obsessed society. But those who share this theology need to recognize that it is one-sided; it ignores the portions of scripture which acknowledge that it is from God that all our blessings flow. And how can blessings from God's creation be evil? And are they evil even when we use them for good? "Wealth," says Peter Gomes, "is not evil, but it is a problem."

Another motto on the other end of the spectrum is, "God Wills My Wealth," or "My Pennies Are From Heaven." Can you see a drawing on the front of a $10.00 bill showing pennies falling from heaven onto a celebrating couple with two children and a dog in front of their mansion as showers of pennies cover the perfectly coifed, leafless lawn?

Have you heard this on prime time airways? It's there on Christian television and radio. It is hard to miss. Jim Bakker, Rex Humbard, and Oral Roberts might have money marked in this way. The "Gospel of Wealth" arose first in the late '70s as a reaction to Sider and Wallis' claim that "wealth is evil" which, of course, made the rich squirm and sweat with guilt. While "God Wills My Wealth" has its basis in several biblical texts, it is also one-sided and can easily fall into a convenient and comforting message for the wealthy who will smile and turn somersaults (and give money to the broadcast) to know that a verse or two out of the Bible justifies their affluent lifestyle. It is true that:

- God grants Solomon riches, possessions, and honor as a reward for his wisdom.
- And God promises to Abraham riches in the promised land for all his children's children.
- God blesses Job with riches as a reward for being faithful.

But there is something wrong with this picture. This theology of money is also one-sided and misinterprets selected texts. This thinking can cause the poor to stumble as they wonder what they have done wrong, since it appears that God has not blessed them financially. It denies that God's creation and God's blessings are for all and it gives the blessing a higher value than the Blessor. In this Gospel of Wealth perspective, the motto *In God We Trust* risks being rubbed down, or out. Riches may impede our trust in God.

These two theological positions are on the extremes, and I have described them as such for emphasis. Actually we would find constellations around each, and other nuanced positions as one moves to the center.

So ... I invite you to evaluate this motto. It is a more balanced one, and it falls in the center of that continuum: "Neither poverty nor riches."

This biblically derived perspective offers us a more difficult challenge as it is easier to be at the extremes than to hold the tension of the center. This middle eastern wisdom includes a larger sweep of the whole biblical witness and is more in sync with Reformed theology. It takes the best from the two opposing positions and neither denies nor inflates the value of wealth.

In an unpublished thesis, the Reverend Mark Vermaire, former pastor of Sherman Street Christian Reformed Church of Grand Rapids, Michigan, commends to the church of today the Prayer of Agur. Found in Proverbs, Chapter 30, this prayer, the only prayer in this collection of Proverbs, reflects both the wisdom of the ancient sage and the deep piety of the Old Testament. It is a remarkably relevant prayer for the Christian in the late twentieth century ("A Presentation and Critical Evaluation of Contemporary Evangelical Perspectives on Wealth," Mark D. Vermaire, Department of Systematic Theology, Calvin College, 1989). Listen to the words of this ancient writer addressing God (or read along with me from Proverbs 30:7-9):

> *Two things I ask of you, do not deny them to me before I die:*
> *Remove far from me falsehood and lying;*
> *give to me neither poverty nor riches;*
> *feed me with the food that I need,*
> *or I shall be full, and deny you, and say, "Who is the Lord?"*
> *or I shall be poor, and steal, and profane the name of my God.*

In essence, the writer confesses a desire to trust God and to live out, as well as to state, that God is the object of trust. The writer wants to be honest and truthful, but recognizes that relationships with money may be problematic: wealth and poverty are roadblocks.

Let us look at both roadblocks.

First, the rich are tempted to rely on their wealth, rather than on God, and thus to deny God's goodness. C. S. Lewis quipped that it is possible for a camel to pass through the eye of a needle, but it hurts the camel!

As the Christmas season is upon us, my thoughts go to Charles Dickens' *A Christmas Carol* with his protagonist, the miser Scrooge. Scrooge is so attached to his possessions that even at Christmas he refuses to give to the poor and hungry, even when his employees plead with him. "They are not my business," he says. "It is enough for a man to understand his own business and to not interfere with other people's. Mine occupies me constantly." May any of us just so occupied with our own business — always striving for a better job, working longer hours, obsessing over interest rates — pray to be startled like Scrooge by midnight ghosts and yield to the possibility of transformation in the new year.

Those who have received much from the hand of God, of them much will be expected: (1) ultimate trust in God, not imagined security of money; (2) generosity, as we are stewards of God's gifts, not their ultimate owner; (3) detachment from possessions, so that were those riches lost, God would not be trusted any less. And those are among the times when the camel pauses and wonders if it will be worth the hurt. This prayer verbalizes the writer's fear that honesty and justice will be compromised if riches flow. In Thomas Jefferson's words, "I have never observed where one's honesty is increased with his riches."

In contrast to the rich, the hungry or poor who have not received the food that they need may run low on patience and begin to mistrust God's goodness and promises, perhaps even steal, and curse God. God does not will poverty for anyone.

Here my thinking turns to Jean-Paul Jean, in *Les Miserables*, who as a hungry, just-released criminal, steals a loaf of bread from a shop window. If we who are living "comfortably" in luxury by global standards fail to share our abundance with those who have to steal for a loaf of bread, we are guilty of (1) greed, and (2) perhaps causing our brother or sister to stumble in faith, and (3) not taking seriously our part in the fulfillment of the prayer we all pray, "Give us this day our daily bread."

"Give me neither poverty nor riches" — make me content to trust in God! And until we sit with God in the New Age — that age where all will be fed and satisfied, where no child will die in infancy, and no laborer will be without a home, where no farmer will go hungry — until then, a part of our trusting in God is to work with God on that very agenda. To be a trusting disciple following the plan of God with not only our spiritual lives but with and through our financial lives.

So what about that phrase on our currency, *In God We Trust*? Do you trust God more than the money on which that motto is printed?

Friends, until that day when Christ rules and *In God We Trust* exemplifies truth, and we trust money less than riches,

> *Give to me neither poverty nor riches;*
> *feed me with the food that I need,*
> *or I shall be full and deny you and say, "Who is the Lord?"*
> *or I shall be poor, and steal, and profane the name of my God.*

Amen.

Vision 2000 And Beyond: What Does Money Have To Do With It?

Deuteronomy 14:22-29; John 12:1-8

Riley E. Jensen

This morning I feel a little like the famous Methodist preacher, Clovis Chapell, who once told a group of clergy at an inter-faith meeting that fall was his favorite season of the year. He enjoyed it because it was stewardship season, and he liked preaching about money. The audience of clergy was amazed to hear a colleague claim to like preaching stewardship sermons. Then he went on to say, "I like to see the generous enjoy it and the stingy squirm."

Now you need to know that my motives are not quite that perverse. While I share Dr. Chapell's feelings about the importance of stewardship and financial giving, I am not as quick to divide my congregation in such a polarizing way. From a Christian perspective, the importance of financial giving goes well beyond the categories of generosity and stinginess. My joy in the subject comes from seeing the enlightenment of people who start connecting giving with God.

When that starts to happen, a healthy church budget is only the by-product of something of much greater consequence — our relationship with God. As we look toward our future, there is a connection with money — how we view it and how we use it. And so I raise the question this morning, "What does money have to do with it?" knowing that it must have a lot to do with it, because Jesus talked more about money than any other subject in his ministry.

How many of you have thought about this subject enough to have adopted a personal philosophy of the use of money? Someone shared with me something he came across in *Forbes* magazine having to do with the philosophy of Dennis Bakke, 51, co-founder and chief executive of AES Corp., an Arlington, Virginia, power generation company: "Everything we have is not ours, it is the Lord's," says Bakke. "We're just stewards of it." Eldest son Brett's reaction: "My father doesn't even think it's his. I'm a little more along the line that it is his. But nowhere did it get to be mine. It's twice removed."

That particular philosophy, while being familiar church talk, is really a radical notion from which certain other things follow if we try to connect our use of money with our Christian commitment. I believe there is such a thing as having the courage of your platitudes so I am going to recite a few to you.

I. We Don't Give To A Budget

First, we don't give to a budget. And if you believe that one, I have a bridge I would like to sell you. Of course, we give to a budget, because our budget reflects our stewardship and our priorities. I can't imagine a congregation in which so many of you crunch numbers for a living not being interested in budgets.

But there is a difference between giving to a budget and giving to a mission. Within days of her tragic death, hundreds of millions of dollars were raised for a trust fund to support Princess Diana's favorite charities. No prospectus was available, no annual reports, not even a mission statement save the desire to continue her good works, and the money flooded in from all over the world — all of it out of a desire to support everything good that Diana stood for.

Is the Church of Jesus Christ any different? We know what Jesus stood for and it is our mission to keep that going. We have 2,000 years of history in which we have changed the world with deeds of love and mercy. Hospitals and schools and churches witness to lives that have been changed and healed. Countless other seeds have been planted because Christians were on the scene to make a sacrificial difference.

In 1992, *Independent Sector* published an interesting report on "Giving and Volunteering in the United States," and it came up with this fairly obvious conclusion: "... the pattern persists that respondents who reported both household contributions and volunteer activities gave more than those who did not volunteer."

Now we know that, don't we? When we invest time and energy, there is value added and our money follows. When some churches hear that, they get excited about increasing volunteerism in the church in the hope that it will have a positive impact on the budget. Friends, I have to tell you that as badly as we need volunteers in all aspects of our church life, that is a weak strategy and a poor understanding of the mission of the church.

The fact of the matter is there is a difference between volunteers and disciples. Volunteers are recruited; disciples are called. Volunteers are doing their duty; disciples are using their gifts. Volunteers are supporting a parochial cause; disciples are giving to a universal mission. Volunteers get burned out; disciples are renewed by a power beyond themselves. Volunteers give as long as their interest lasts; disciples give as long as their life shall last.

You see, money is not merely something we carry in our pockets. It is the extension of our personalities. It is also an indicator of where our commitments really lie, and the use we make of it determines the ends our lives will serve. Ultimately, we don't give to a budget; we give to what we believe in.

That is why our New Testament lesson is one of the most controversial in the Bible. Judas, who was the treasurer for the disciples, accused Mary of wasting money. That expensive perfume could have been sold to support some line item in the budget, but Mary's satisfaction came in giving it away in gratitude for the presence of her Lord, and in turn Jesus applauded the depth of her giving.

II. We Give Because We Need To Give

Secondly, we give because we need to give. An old friend used to say, "If we don't have charity in our hearts, we have the worst kind of heart trouble." The fact of the matter is that we need to give more than the Lord needs our gifts.

One of the most misunderstood biblical guidelines for giving is the tithe. If you have been around the church for any length of time, you have heard about it and maybe you have even done it. Our Old Testament lesson is but one of several passages that seems to lift up the tithe as the pattern for giving. Here the tenth of the agricultural products and the firstborn of the herds and flocks — or the equivalent in money — is to be taken to the central sanctuary two years out of three. There it is to be consumed in sacred feasts before the Lord. These feasts are meant to remind God's people that the land is God's and that all good things come from God's hands. At the end of the third year the tithe is to be kept in the areas where it was produced and is to be distributed to the landless and the poor.

Now the biblical passages on tithing have often been read and interpreted to mean that the tithe is simply a tax to support the religious establishment, or the benefit of tithing is held up to show that the prosperity of the giver is a reward for tithing.

Wrong! Here the tithe is seen as an act of worship. First, in an agriculturally-based economy it is turned into a giant potluck supper where everyone gathers to eat the tithe of food and produce in thanksgiving for God's goodness. And then one use, though not the exclusive use, was to feed the less fortunate. Clearly, part of the tithe evolved into a sort of temple tax to support the priesthood, but that is not held up as its highest and best purpose.

In scripture, the tithe has less to do with a magic formula that will satisfy a religious obligation than evidence of a person's connection to God. Therefore, giving at its foundation is spiritual rather than economic. As we learn to give, we grow in our relationship to God.

It is common to think of a philanthropist as someone who donates large sums of money. In fact, the word is derived from two Greek words, *philos* which means "loving" and *anthropos* which means "man." The two together mean "a loving man or woman." This means that everyone who gives in love is a philanthropist, regardless of the amount given.

However one looks at it, giving is a matter of the heart. When your heart is right toward God, you will give of your time and talent and treasure. The amount matters less than your desire to do so.

III. We Have To Start Somewhere

This leads to my final platitude. "We have to start somewhere." Because we live in an institutional context and because many of us are still learning about what giving means in our relationship with God, we naturally want some further guidance. A frequently asked question from new members is, "How much am I expected to give?" And the answer, "That's between you and God," is not entirely satisfactory for some people.

If you are going to give, if you want to give, where do you start? I want to leave you with the point that tithing as an act of worship is so much more than the number ten. Let me share a short story.

The treasurer of a congregation resigned. The elders asked a man who managed the local grain elevator to take his position. He agreed under two conditions: (1) that no report from the treasurer be required for one whole year; and (2) that no one ask him any questions during the one-year period. The elders gulped, but finally agreed, since he was a trusted person in the community and well-known and because most of them did business with him as manager of the elevator.

At the year's end he gave his report: the indebtedness of $25,000 on the church was paid. The parsonage had been redecorated. The pastor's salary had been increased. Mission giving was up 200 percent. There were no outstanding bills, and there was a cash balance of $12,000.

Immediately, a shocked congregation that had been used to barely making ends meet asked, "What happened?" Quietly he responded: "Most of you bring your grain to my elevator. As you did business with me I simply withheld ten percent on your behalf and gave it to the church in your name, and *you never missed it!*"

We know that it is only a parable, because if it really happened the lawsuits would be flying. The point is that we have to start somewhere. While some of us feel that the number ten is the right number, it is not a number Jesus lays on us. Nor is it a number the Apostle Paul, the great fundraiser and stewardship preacher of the early church, even mentions once.

But what he does say in 1 Corinthians 16:2 is: "On the first day of the week, each one of you is to put something aside and store it up, so you may prosper." The principles are: Give regularly, give proportionately, and give to God first.

In the freedom Christ gives us, we are responsible for fixing our own percentage. God knows that some of us have heavy obligations while others of us are relatively free of the kind of obligations we once had.

I keep remembering a baseball story that is relevant during this World Series month and as we reflect on our stewardship commitments. Charlie Grimm was the manager of the Chicago Cubs at the time. The Cubs were having a disastrous year and were in a long losing streak. But one day in the midst of that miserable slump, one of Grimm's scouts phoned excitedly from the hinterlands: "Charlie, Charlie," he shouted with joy. "I've just seen the greatest pitcher in the country! He pitched a perfect no-hit, no-run game! Twenty-seven strikeouts! No one even hit a foul ball off him until there were two out in the ninth. I've got him here now. What shall I do?"

"Sign the guy that got the foul," said Grimm. "Our club needs hitters!" And that's what God needs, and that's what the church needs, people who will step up to the plate and start somewhere.

A Tip Or A Tithe

Genesis 28:10-22

Jeffrey D. Weenink

Introduction

A minister was walking along the beach one day and stumbled upon a lamp. Picking it up and wiping it off caused the lamp to shake and smoke and a genie came out. The genie thanked the minister for this new-found freedom after years of captivity and offered him one wish.

The minister immediately said, "I've always wanted to visit the Holy Land but I am afraid of flying. Even in those Concordes as safe as they are, I just can't bring myself to fly. And I get seasick thinking about boats. Why, even an ocean liner as smooth as the QE2 makes me queasy. So could you build a highway across the ocean so that I could drive to the Holy Land?"

The genie looked at him in surprise and shock and replied, "You must be kidding. Do you realize the engineering challenges that would have to be overcome to achieve that feat? Even I have limitations. Can't you think of anything else to wish for?"

The minister thought for a few minutes and then said, "Okay. I know what I want. I wish for all the members of the congregation I serve to become tithers." To that the genie replied, "Do you want that to be a two-lane or four-lane highway?"

A Modern Parable

Now it came to pass that a certain couple invited some friends to a popular restaurant. The food was good and the waiter most efficient. When they had finished, the host wrote out the tip on the credit card slip. As they left, the waiter smiled happily, which meant that the tip was satisfactory, even generous. Most are familiar with such customs — and they are good. The standard tip for service is fifteen percent. According to Hilda Klinkenberg, a consultant with

Etiquette International and author of *At Ease — Professionally*, the tipping standard is rapidly rising to twenty percent.

But when the hosts filled their offering envelope it dawned on them that they paid a waiter for two hours of enjoyment, four times what they were giving God in their weekly envelope. They gave unto the waiter the tithe, but unto God they gave leftovers. So lie the ironies of how many make their response to God for all the goodness served and heaped upon us so freely.

That perhaps is why a wise person once said, "Surely there is something wrong with our standard of values, when we compare what we spend for incidentals or amusements and what we return unto almighty God."

A tip or a tithe? For Jacob there was no hesitation in what his response to God's abiding presence would be. For us it seems to have become a more difficult decision. Jacob's story, you remember, is not about a saint so holy that he awakes to find himself in the presence of God because of his good actions. It is the story of a scoundrel who awakes with a startling sense of wonder as he realizes that God had visited him in his dreams in spite of all the mistakes he had made.

Jacob was in a bit of a jam because the choices he had made turned out to be selfish, calculating, and dishonest. His conniving had caught up with him. He had deceived his aged father, cheated his brother Esau, and was running for his life to escape the consequences. It is on the first night of his flight into the wilderness that he finds himself pursed not by Esau but by the grace of God. He has a vision of a ladder to heaven with angels ascending and descending. As the Lord stood beside him and said, "Know that I am with you and will keep you wherever you go ..." (Genesis 28:15). In amazement Jacob murmurs, "Surely the Lord is in this place; and I did not know it!" (Genesis 28:17).

Jacob's situation is symbolic of the human condition threefold: a wrong relation to things (our material world), a wrong relation to people (deceitful, dishonest dealings), a wrong relation to God (a low awareness of God's presence and outright disobedience). Yet, because of his vision, Jacob begins to see all he is and has as a gift from God. He promises to use the stone which was the pillow for his head as the foundation for a pillar in the up-building of God's house. Then he says, "... and of all that you give me I will surely give one tenth to you" (Genesis 28:22b). Here lies one of the many biblical affirmations for what is known as a tithe.

A Tithe

We usually think of the tithe as that form of legalism that was abolished by the advent of the Christian era. The general assumption in many quarters of the contemporary church is that the tithe is an expression of an archaic demand, not the grace-filled redemption of the liberating Christ. Instead of a threatening ultimatum upon a fearful people or a capricious requirement for impoverished nomads, the title was a plan for salvation and security for a precarious, fragile nation. It set Israel apart from the barbarous and callous cultures that sought to engulf and destroy them in the land of promise. It was a gift from God rather than an extraction of gifts. Douglas Johnson in his insightful volume *The Tithe: Challenge or Legalism?* insists: "That the tithe of the Old Testament is a testimony to the interconnectedness of people and God. It incorporates a cycle of giving and receiving and using. It signifies a relationship that can't be content with using a strict formula from the past. The tithe, like the message of the Old Testament, is a living witness of God." Tithing therefore is not driven by legalistic compulsion, but rather arises as the spiritual response of a thankful soul.

I realize for many this topic is about as welcome as a snowstorm in June. The biblical concept of the tithe is often understood as an ancient, archaic, legalistic intrusion into our lives, which is compulsory and restrictive, painful to ponder and inappropriate for pastors to preach.

Hearing about it hits home. We are like the farmer who was asked if he had 200 cows would he give twenty to God? "Yes, of course!" he said. "If you had 100 cows would you give ten to God?" "I most certainly would," was his response. "If you had ten cows would you give one to God?" "Now that's not fair," he said. "You know I only have ten cows!"

Our faith does not deny that economics has a place in the human condition. By the same token it was Martin Luther who said that a religion that gives nothing, costs nothing, and suffers nothing, is worth nothing.

Tithing places before us a standard by which we may center our lives in gratitude to God. Tithing doesn't have anything to do with raising a budget or supporting a program. It has everything to do with making a spiritual response to God. Jacob's story is timeless and relevant because it describes how this impoverished soul chose to respond.

If the church exists simply to meet our needs we become nothing less than beggars. The ministry of Jesus Christ is broader than that, my integrity as a pastor goes deeper than that, the biblical witness sends forth a spiritual message bigger than that.

Tithing is not a barter with God. It is not a financial contract assuring an increase in profits if one participates. It isn't a mathematical formula for assuring the presence of God, nor a clever device for lining the coffers of the church. To tithe is essentially and fundamentally a testimony of faith in the creativity and goodness of God. What we do with what we have can be an outward and visible sign of God's inward and redeeming grace alive and well within us. This is when the distribution of what we have becomes sacramental.

Conclusion

Do you know that studies actually verify that the more money we make, the smaller percentage we give to the church. That's right! In other words, the biggest percentage givers to our church are those who have the smallest income. I don't say that to embarrass anyone. It's a fact. The biggest percentage givers in your church are not the big salaried people with fine jobs, as you might guess, but the average member, and in some instances you would be thrilled to know what some of our retired people are giving, and others who are on limited incomes.

Many will be able to resonate with the story of a man who pledged years ago to tithe all that he made to the work of the Lord. His first week's paycheck was $50 and so he tithed $5 that week.

As he grew older and more prosperous, he got $100 a week, then $200 a week — over $10,000 a year. All during this time, he continued to tithe, until he finally rose to $500 a week. Then one day he called his pastor and said, "I've got to talk to you." The pastor came to the man's beautiful home. They had a good time talking about old times, and finally the man came to the point. "You remember that promise I made years ago to tithe? How can I get released from it? It's like this," the man continued. "When I made that promise I had to give only $5, but now I'm giving $500 a week to fulfill that pledge."

The old pastor thought for a moment, and then said to his friend, "I'm afraid we cannot get you released from that promise, but there is something we can do for you. We can kneel and ask God to shrink your income so you can afford to tithe $5 once more."

A tip or a tithe? In the context of your own relation to God in Christ, you must decide. This is my prediction: if you do decide to accept the tithe as a standard, you will be beginning a grand Christian adventure in faith. Furthermore, you will be amazed as to how happy you are on the other nine-tenths.

Therefore, as I use God's word for my guide, I find that the principle is valid as a starting point in my faith journey. In giving a proportion and a tenth as a guide, I have been spiritually comfortable knowing that I have not robbed God. Moreover, I have been emotionally comfortable knowing that, no matter how large a budget or campaign, my share of the burden is simply God's share of my income. Finally, I have been physically comfortable, knowing from experience that our household gets along better on the nine-tenths of our blessings than we ever could with one-tenth more without God's benediction.

Stewardship's Toughest Question

2 Corinthians 9:6-7

Daniel G. Nicely

Introduction
And God stepped out on space,
And He looked around and said:
"I'm lonely — I'll make me a world."
And as far as the eye of God could see
Darkness covered everything,
Blacker than a hundred midnights down in a cypress swamp.
Then God smiled, and the light broke,
And the darkness rolled up on one side,
And the light stood shining on the other;
And God said: "That's good!"
Then God reached out and took the light in His hands,
And God rolled the light around in His hands
Until He made the sun; and He set that sun
A-blazing in the heavens.
And the light that was left from making the sun God gathered
It up in a shining ball and flung it against the darkness,
Spangling the night with the moon and stars.
Then down between the darkness and the light he hurled the world,
And God said: "That's good!"
Then God himself stepped down — and the sun was on His right hand,
And the moon was on His left;
The stars were clustered about His head,
And the earth was under His feet.
And God walked, and where He trod
His footsteps hollowed the valleys out
And bulged the mountains up:
Then He stopped and looked and saw that the earth
Was hot and barren.

So God stepped over to the edge of the world
And He spat out the seven seas
He batted His eyes, and the lights flashed —
He clapped His hands and the thunder rolled —
And the waters above the earth came down,
The cooling waters came down.
Then the green grass sprouted,
And the little red flowers blossomed,
The pine tree pointed his finger to the sky,
And the oak spread out his arms,
The lakes cuddled down in the hollows of the ground,
And the rivers ran down to the sea; and God smiled again,
And the rainbow appeared, and curled itself around His shoulder.
Then God raised His arm and He waved His hand over the sea
And over the land, and He said: "Bring forth! Bring forth!"
And quicker than God could drop His hands, fishes, and fowls
And beasts and birds swam the rivers and the seas,
Roamed the forests and the woods,
And split the air with their wings, and God said: "That's good!"
Then God walked
Around and God looked around on all that He had made.
He looked at His sun, and He looked at His moon,
And He looked at His little stars;
He looked on His world with all its living things,
And God said: "I'm lonely still."
Then God sat down on the side of a hill where He could think.
By a deep, wide river He sat down with His head in His hands.
God thought and thought, till He thought:
"I'll make me a man!" Up from the bed of the river God scooped
    the clay;
And by the bank of the river He kneeled Him down;
And there the great God Almighty, who lit the sun and fixed it in
    the sky,
Who flung the stars to the most far corner of the night,
Who rounded the earth in the middle of His hand; this great God,
Like a mammy bending over His baby,
Kneeled down in the dust toiling over a lump of clay

Till He shaped it in His own image,
Then into it He blew the breath of life,
And man became a living soul.
Amen and amen.

The New Testament Lesson is from 2 Corinthians 9:6-7: "The point is this: the one who sows sparingly will also reap sparingly, and the one who sows bountifully will also reap bountifully. Each of you must give as you have made up your mind, not reluctantly or under compulsion, for God loves a cheerful giver."

We remind ourselves of the *Creation Story* from Genesis as written by James Weldon Johnson. God gave all of us two ultimate gifts: The good earth, populated with creatures and food and resources for humankind, so dramatically and poetically written in the Old Testament book of Genesis. Then God's other great gift, Jesus Christ, the New Testament's new covenant.

We can view our pledges and gifts to the church partially as payment of an inheritance tax. Each generation of us, in turn, inherited the good earth and the good Savior.

It wouldn't be much of a bill for our inheritance tax from Christ's earthly possessions. He didn't leave us a home or farm, office building or even a carpenter's shop. No business. There was no life insurance, no stock portfolio, no cars or jewelry. He only left a peasant Jew's clothing of perhaps a loose garment, a girdle or belt, a pair of sandals. As we say, the few clothes on his back. Even they, as you recall, were taken as booty by the soldiers who crucified him, casting lots for his possessions while he was on the cruel cross.

But we did inherit from Christ — grace! — God's rich grace of salvation and a spiritual legacy.

Closer to home, each of us, when we joined this church, inherited what our forebears left us. This church, as you know, has a very rich history of program and service since its founding in 1861, as well as a very rich history of facility.

In my time we've had capital improvement drives in 1976, 1979, 1984, and 1990; and as you know, this year we're completing work on the youth center which is nearly finished. All programs and facilities are part of a rich Christian heritage. My guess is that thirty to forty percent of this congregation has never had the opportunity to participate in one of these so-called modern improvement drives. So stay with us — we'll arrange an opportunity, and you can pay a little more "inheritance tax."

By the right of creation, and by the right of redemption, God is the one and only owner of all. Each of us is a steward and must give an accounting of ourselves. God requires of the steward a constantly recurring recognition of God's ownership of the whole. We are required to set aside a certain part, a certain percentage as our offering — our response to God's generosity.

People sometimes ask me about their "share." Some of the questions most often asked are: If I give a percentage of my income, do I use the gross figure or the after-tax net? (Alas, Caesar is with us always.) The answer is, "Yes," the gross amount. What about tithing? Is that a good idea: The answer is, "Yes." Do I include in my pledge an amount for my capital gains? (The market is down now but most of us remember when the Dow hit 1,000 in 1972, 5,000 in 1995, and 7,000 in 1997.) Basically, we are to give in proportion to what we receive. Count (itemize) your blessings and then give, proportionately!

Recently, I have spent time deciding about a new car. Once past a little "sticker shock" most of the mid-line cars cost about 150 percent of our first home. Then the dreadful decision about two or four doors, cruise, tilt, power windows, power seats, four-wheel or two-wheel drive, keyless entry, trunk release, leather seats, AM-FM stereo cassette, tinted windows, telephone, and other goodies too numerous to mention. Maybe they cost substantially more than 150 percent of our first home because they begin to look like a home.

Speaking of blessings and the "good old days," I remember my first car. I was 22 years old, working on a master's degree, and poor. At the end of a summer job, and living with my parents in Virginia, I found a 1946 four-door Plymouth. It had been a taxi, the motor had been replaced in 1948, and it had 100,000 miles on that engine. With my dear grandmother's help and $200, I bought the car and by God's grace made it back to Princeton. Now, just for comparison, my benevolent giving has increased substantially since I was 22 years old. But probably not proportionate to my present transportation and all my other blessings.

You as a congregation are doing well. Frankly, some of you are doing so well that I sometimes worry more about your physical well-being than your spiritual! Obviously, we want you healthy both physically and spiritually!

Our budget for 1999 is, and I hope all of your read it carefully, $1,351,331! That is a substantial amount for a congregation of 1,350 members. And this is to remind you that our modest endowment fund makes no contribution to the operating budget. You the members contribute ninety percent of the budget. The remaining amount comes from plate offering, non-pledged giving, and special gifts. We are scheduled to give 24 percent of the total budget, or $324,795, to mission outside of Westminster. This is the mission track that Dr. Weenink put us on when he was our interim pastor in 1989-90. He challenged us to add one percent per year until the year 2000 when that budget will give 25 percent to mission. Frankly, some years it has not been easy because each year that mission went up one percent, staff, program, facilities, and administration went down one percent. Obviously, the pie has had to get larger each year to accommodate our growing mission involvement, other programs, and inflation.

Another star in Westminster's crown is that we are the largest benevolence contributor in the presbytery and our total validated mission for denominational causes is the largest of all the 260 Presbyterian churches in the state of Michigan. The average Westminster pledge 1998, this year, is $2,279 — probably one of the highest Presbyterian pledges in the nation, on average. This is not being said to exalt ourselves. It does say what in actuality we are doing. But listen to what a member of the Stewardship Committee tells me.

The Stewardship Committee member reminded me that if Westminster members tithe, that means the average salary in Westminster is $22,791 or about $10.79 an hour. My guess is that, on average, the members of this congregation make substantially more than $10.79 an hour. Considerably more!

I can't remember what I gave away when I was in my early twenties — probably not very much. But the real question for me is: "Do I give now in equal proportion when I compare the automobiles that I drive, the lifestyle I live, the salary I make, and the 'inheritance taxes' that I owe?" It's a question you must ask and answer yourself.

The majority of members pledge and pay. Some even pay in advance, for which we are most grateful. Some pledge and don't pay and that gives us concern about the integrity of making a pledge. Some don't pledge and give regularly and have a history of dependability. Some tithe. Some give proportionate to their income. Some treat the church as a gratuity and give a tip. And, alas, some do nothing. And this raises a question about honoring their vows of church membership.

John and Sylvia Ronsdale, authors of *Behind the Stained-Glass Window*, a book about money dynamics in the church, write: "Personal finance, not sex or politics, is the last taboo topic in America. But as much as the general population is uncomfortable talking about their personal view of money, churchgoers are just as averse to discussing what they consider to be an extremely private subject."

No one here is going to tell you what to give. Stewardship at Westminster is vertical. It is between you, your conscience, your spiritual life, your physical blessings, and your God. You and God have a good conversation about this and decide Stewardship's Toughest Questions: "What is my response? What is my share? What is my inheritance tax? What do I give?" Remember that admonition in the New Testament lesson for today from 2 Corinthians: "Each of you must give as you have made up your mind."

My hope for Westminster is that it would have the missionary zeal of the Methodists, the enthusiasm of the American Black Church, have singing like Welch miners, the fervor in attendance of the Baptists, the compassionate hearts of Jews, the *simpatico* of Puerto Ricans, giving that will surpass the Assemblies of God, and do it all with the distinguished style of Episcopalians.

Now is the time to recognize that God gave us the good earth with all its rich population of food and shelter. Now is the time to be grateful for a loving Savior who came and suffered and died for all of us on the cruel cross. Now is the time to pay that inheritance tax. Now is the time to answer Stewardship's Toughest Question: "What shall I give?"

Listen to the words of one verse of a great hymn:

Were the whole realm of nature mine,
That were a present far too small;
Love so amazing, so divine,
Demands my soul, my life, my all.
    ("When I Survey The Wondrous Cross,"
    Isaac Watts)

All That Is Not Given Is Lost

Luke 12:13-21

William A. Evertsberg

You know what I think? I think there is no such thing as atheists. Atheists don't believe in God, but I don't believe in atheists. I am an a-atheist. I believe that everybody worships something. I believe that everybody worships a god of one sort or another. One way to define "God" is to say that God is the highest good in our particular value system, the supreme person or thing which occupies the pinnacle of our individual universe, that which sits upon the throne of our hearts. Paul Tillich defined "God" as our "ultimate concern." If we define "God" in that way, therefore, we can truthfully say that everyone has one. There is no such thing as an atheist. Nobody worships nothing. There are no atheists in foxholes. And there are no atheists in shopping malls either.

Our "ultimate concern," our God, is whatever possesses the capacity to make us do something we wouldn't ordinarily do. The English word "God" comes from the Old Irish word *gut*, which means "voice." Our God is the voice to which we listen, the power which summons us to travel roads we would ordinarily not travel.

Among all the worthy — and unworthy — claimants to the throne of our lives — nation, family, prestige, fame — none is more persistent and seductive than money. For many of us, money is a voice, and so for many of us, it is the voice of Pavarotti or Domingo. It makes us *do* things. Let me illustrate. The Reverend Ken Barley told me this story. On a particularly strenuous and hectic day, Ken was sitting in his office counting the paper clips when he received a phone call from Mrs. Peabody, a distant acquaintance of his. The secretary said that Ken couldn't be bothered during one of the more important activities of his day, but she was distraught and persistent, so the secretary put her through. She had some heartbreaking news. Fluffy was dead. He said, "Oh,

Mrs. Peabody, I'm so terribly sorry. You must be so upset. Who is Fluffy?"

Mrs. Peabody told him that Fluffy was her beloved French poodle, and that she was calling to see if he would conduct the funeral. In a failed effort to disguise his offended dignity, the Reverend Mr. Barley said: "Mrs. Peabody, I am a Presbyterian minister with a Master's Degree in theology. I do *not* do funerals for French poodles."

On the other end of the line there was a fresh flood of tears. "Well, Mr. Barley, whatever am I going to do? We simply must lay Fluffy to rest in a fitting manner. Do you know of another clergyperson who will help us out?"

The Reverend Mr. Barley ran through his mental catalogue of local ministers and finally said, "Why don't you try the Methodist minister down the street? He'll probably do it for you."

Mrs. Peabody said, "Oh, thank you very much, Mr. Barley. You've been very helpful. And, oh, just one more thing. Do you think it would be all right if I offered the Methodist minister a small gift? I was thinking of $500." There was a long, long silence on Mr. Barley's end of the phone. Finally, he said, "Mrs. Peabody, why didn't you tell me the dog was a Presbyterian?"

Nothing like a little cold cash to encourage us to jettison our integrity, is there? It could even make you conduct a funeral for a French poodle. In his play *Richard III*, Shakespeare puts it this way: "Gold were as good as twenty orators, and will no doubt, tempt him to anything."

Jesus knows this. That's why he talks more about money than about any other single reality in the Christian life. G. K. Chesterton said, "There is one thing that Christ and all the Christian saints have said with a sort of savage monotony: they have said simply that to be rich is to be in peculiar danger of moral wreck." That's an interesting way of putting it, right? The way we use our money, or in some cases, the way our money uses us, is the single most important indicator about who or what sits on the throne of our lives. With a kind of savage monotony, Jesus makes a pest of himself saying the same thing over and over again. He sounds like a broken record or, to bring the image a little more up-to-date, like a stuck CD player. Especially in the Gospel of Luke, where Jesus' so-called "preference for the poor" is especially prominent, Jesus' laser beam seems to get perpetually stuck along the same track of the compact disc, and the message of the track is this: "Be careful whom you worship. Be careful about your ultimate concern. Watch that voice, or *gut*, or God, you listen to most persistently."

Someone once calculated that there are 500 verses in the Bible about prayer, and 500 about faith, but over 2,000 about money. And since Jesus keeps saying it over and over again, I am asking you on this Stewardship Sunday to consider the truth of the statement I've taken this morning: "All that is not given is lost."

Some of you will recognize where that title comes from. That statement appears on the first page of a book by Dominique Lapierre called *The City of Joy*. Later they made a movie out of the book, by the same title, and that statement appears as the last scene of the movie: "All that is not given is lost." Do you remember it? *The City of Joy* is about a rickshaw puller from the streets of Calcutta, India, a man named Hasari Pal. He probably earned in his entire lifetime less than some of us in this room make in a single day, but lived a life richer and more meaningful, I venture to guess, than most of us will ever dare to dream. After a lifetime of scraping together a few cents a day, Hasari Pal discovers what he considers to be a profound truth about human life: "All that is not given is lost."

Consider that statement with me for a few moments, would you? I am not asking you to *believe* it, only to *consider* it. Because frankly, I'm not so sure I believe it myself, and even if I believe it, I don't live it. In my better moments I believe it, but at other times it does not seem quite true that what I keep for myself is lost to me. I rather enjoy the things I keep for myself. On Friday I took a break from writing this sermon to go and buy another armful of books and a couple of CD's (compact discs, not cash deposits). And I am tempted to refute Hasari Pal and say that "all that is not kept is lost." That seems closer to my motto: "All that is not kept is lost."

And so after long neglect I find it helpful to reacquaint myself with the words of Jesus of Nazareth, Jesus the guerilla preacher who is always terrorizing us with all these little surprise attack parables. This time it is the Parable of the Rich Fool. Notice with me for a few moments the exquisite art with which Jesus and Luke get their point across in this little parable. First we notice that the rich fool has almost casually kicked the God of Israel off the throne of his heart and put something else in its place. The parable tells us that "the land of the rich man produced abundantly." In other words, the rich fool was the fortunate recipient of an extravagant generosity, but then promptly ignored that inconvenient little fact. Oh, I know he worked hard. He'd studied agriculture; he'd studied the logistics of production, transportation, and marketing. He was engaged in a process of sound long-term investing and sensible long-range planning. He worked like a dog and saved like a miser; he was a good Republican.

But he'd forgotten that his prolificity was an undeserved gift from the hand of a glad God: "The land of the rich man produced abundantly." Not the rich man himself, but his land, God's land. Blessed with soil, crops, and weather almost miraculous in productivity, the man never once pauses to acknowledge his indebtedness to the giver of sun, rain, and growth. George Buttrick says that "he was carried to fortune on a fecundity, a light, a heat, a constancy of nature's cycles, which are boundless mysteries of blessing — and he called them 'mine.' "

"He called them 'mine.' " And having ignored God, the source of his good fortune, he then neglects what should have been its end and goal — the common good. He seems to have forgotten that extravagant surplus is to be shared, not hoarded. He seems to have forgotten that "to whom much has been given, much will be required." Notice what he says to himself. He says, "What should I do, for I have no place to store my crops." Notice. Notice that when we have too much, we're always sensible but selfishly looking for places to hide the surplus. I don't know about you, but when I have too much, which, incidentally, isn't too often, I'm not often asking how I can give it away, but where I can sock it away for my retirement. Likewise with the rich fool. But back in the fourth century Saint Ambrose pointed out that the rich man didn't need bigger barns. If he had only looked around at his neighbors, he would have noticed that he had adequate storage for his grain in the mouths of the needy.

The rich fool forgot two important entities in his world: God and neighbor. He'd forgotten the Great Commandment: Love God above all and your neighbor as yourself. But now notice what happens to a man or a woman who forgets those two important realities in the world: she or he is left all alone. Buttrick points out that this man has 61 words worth of dialogue, or rather monologue, in this parable, and that among them, the words "I," "me," and "mine" appear twelve times. There is thought for neither God nor neighbor in his little speech.

Bereft of God and neighbor, the rich fool has no one with whom to rejoice over his great good fortune, and no one with whom to discuss what to do about his admittedly enviable problem of inadequate storage. There is no one to talk to but himself. He says, "And I will say to myself, 'Self, you have ample goods laid up for many years; Self, you done good! You deserve a break today! Relax, take yourself out to dinner. Go on a vacation.'"

The thing is, there's no one with whom to go out to dinner or on vacation, since the story mentions no friends or family, this poor rich fool, the Howard Hughes of the first century. Ken Baily says that the rich fool "has the money to buy a vacuum and live in it." At the end of the story, he is rich, alone, foolish, and dead. Jesus says, "You fool! Life is short. You can never tell when it's going to end. Didn't you know that? And the things you have prepared for yourself, whose will they be?" If you are not rich toward God, whose will they be?

Do you understand his mistake? Do you? He was listening to the wrong voice, in Old Irish, the wrong *gut*, the wrong God. He listened instead to the seductive siren song of that great but penultimate good called security. We are peaceless, restless creatures. We know life is uncertain and fortune whimsical and arbitrary. So we place our trust in larger barns or in long-term slow growth international mutual funds.

In a prosperous society like ours, you see, the greatest danger is always that people will worship the wrong god, and sell their souls to the wrong buyer. Money is not what we want and not what we need. In his *Divine Comedy*, Dante says it one way. In Dante's "Inferno," the fourth circle of hell is reserved for those who spent their earthly lives misusing their money, and of these poor souls Dante says, "For all the gold the moon looks down upon could of these weary souls give rest to none." And in the film *Field of Dreams*, Archie Moonlight Graham says the same thing in different words. "It's money they have and peace they lack." In an interview with *The Wall Street Journal* one time, John Updike said a very interesting thing. He said, "The word 'enough' is one of those words Americans have a very hard time learning." The word is "enough."

So, teachers as different as Jesus, Hasari Pal, Shakespeare, Dante, and Archie Moonlight Graham keep reminding us of something we all know but keep forgetting: that life grows deeper and shines brighter not by what we get, but by what we give. In a society which has tried desperately to place King Dollar on the throne of our hearts, a prodigious, unrelenting pressure has been brought to bear upon us to believe that the more we have, the more we live. Which is simply not true. It is perhaps the most persistent and titanic lie ever perpetrated on American society. The simple truth is this: The more we give, the more we live.

I want to end with an ancient story. It's kind of a counter-parable to this one. It's about Jewish farmers with big barns. It was told centuries ago by the Jewish rabbis, and it has been told and retold in numberless forms since then. Probably you have heard it, but it is too beautiful to be left untold this morning.

There was a man who had two sons. He was a successful farmer, and when he died, he left his land to his two sons. Over the course of time, one of the sons married a young woman and raised a family of six children. The other son remained single. The two young men farmed the land together, and everything they harvested, they divided equally. The grain was placed in two barns, one for each brother.

They grew older. The land was good, and the weather kind. They prospered, and both began to plan for their old age. One night while going over his accounts the unmarried brother began thinking to himself, "My brother has seven mouths to feed, and I am all alone. He will need a bigger share of the crops than I need. But he will never agree to accept a bigger share of the harvest." He thought and thought and finally decided what to do.

Late one night, long after his brother had fallen asleep, the unmarried brother got out of bed, walked to the barn, and began carrying sacks of grain to his brother's barn.

Meanwhile — ah, aren't these Jewish stories great; you already know what happened, don't you? Meanwhile, the married brother was planning ahead as well. He said to himself, "My brother and I are getting older. But I have been blessed with a wife and six children to take care of me when I am old. My brother has no one. He will need more than his share to store up against old age. But he will never agree to accept a larger share of the harvest."

And so this brother too got up in the dead of night while his brother was asleep and went out to the barn and began to carry sacks of grain to his brother's barn. This went on for several nights, each brother removing some of his grain to his brother's barn, so that every morning, the two piles were of equal size. They couldn't figure it out. It was a miracle. Every morning both brothers would go to the barn and say to themselves, "Didn't I carry 1,000 pounds of grain to my brother's barn last night? What happened?"

Then one night, when the moon was full, the brothers met in a field midway between the two barns. And when they saw each other and realized what the other brother had been doing, they began to weep, dropped their sacks, and embraced.

The rabbis tell us that just then clouds drifted across the face of the shining moon, and it began to rain.

Do you know what this was? Do you know what it was? It was the tears of God, weeping for joy, because two of his children had finally — finally — gotten the point.

Do you get the point? Do you get the point? All that is not given is lost.

Dispensers Of The Magnificently Varied Grace Of God

1 Peter 4:10

Allan J. Weenink

One rainy Sunday afternoon, two children had difficulty entertaining themselves, until they stumbled on the idea of acting out their church school lesson of the morning. The little boy agreed he would be Noah and his sister could be Mrs. Noah. They found an old cardboard box which they decided would be an ideal "ark" and filled it with their toy animals.

The bathtub seemed the logical place for their "flood." They turned off the electric light — "and the sun disappeared." Then they turned on the shower and "the floods descended." After some time they turned off the shower, "and the rains ceased and the ark floated on the waters." They pushed the wall switch "and the sun reappeared." They pulled the plug of the bathtub "and the floods receded until the ark once more rested on dry ground." Mission completed — scripture fulfilled.

There was another part to the story, however. Noah and his wife had offered a sacrifice of thanksgiving to the Lord, and the Lord was pleased. The children decided the kitchen stove would be the place for them to burn the sacrifice. Reaching into the ark the little boy found one of his sister's animals and said, "Let's sacrifice this — it would make a good gift for God." "Oh, no," cried his sister in alarm, "I couldn't part with that." Then reaching into the ark she found one of her brother's animals and said, "Here, let's give this to God instead."

Her brother was unwilling to agree to that. They pondered for some time, for it was an agonizing decision — what to offer to the Lord as an expression of praise and sacrifice of thanksgiving for all God's blessings. Suddenly the little girl had a happy thought. Scampering off to the attic, she returned with an old toy lamb. It had only three legs, its head was battered, it had no tail and was so dirty no one could guess its real color. "Here," she cried in relief at the apparently easy solution to the difficult problem, "let's give this to God. We will never want it again." And so they made their "sacrifice" of thanksgiving, comfortable with themselves that they had truly honored God.

We find humor in the story and smile at the whimsical antics and ingenuity of children who play their games with biblical stories. Inadvertently, however, children have a way of getting at the truth. And the truth is that God has often been blessed by humanity's leftovers. And sacrifice has been, in reality, a sharing of what we think we can get by with.

That of course is not the way Peter looked at it when he wrote: "Like good stewards of the manifold grace of God, serve one another with whatever gift each of you has received" (1 Peter 4:10). Because we have been recipients of the extraordinary generosity of God's free grace we are called upon to serve one another with the same grace that God has bestowed on us. "Dispensers of the magnificently varied grace of God," as J. B. Phillips translates it, offers a new perspective on humanity's response to the infinite variety of God's bounty. We do not administer God's manifold grace but we are permitted the unbelievable privilege of serving as good stewards, guardians, and dispensers of the gifts of that grace.

It begins in the Old Testament with the psalmist chanting: "What shall I return to the Lord for all his bounty to me? I will take up the cup of salvation and call on the name of the Lord, I will pay my vows to the Lord in the presence of all his people ... I will offer to you a thanksgiving sacrifice and call on the name of the Lord" (Psalm 116:12-14, 17).

The meaning of our dispensership stewardship, comes to its fulfillment in the New Testament. Paul says it is putting into practice God's plan for our lives and that "our very giving proves the reality of our faith." Christian stewardship is simply Christian faith in intelligent and responsible action. It is the mark of one's faith. It is the believer's response to God's mercies. Our Lord summed it up in one sentence: "From everyone to whom much has been given, much more will be required; and from the one to whom much has been entrusted, even more will be demanded" (Luke 12:48b).

Life is a trust and an assignment from God and we owe God an accounting. This is not a threat, but rather the recognition of reality. It is a fundamental principle of life which we call stewardship — God's ownership and humanity's partnership. Over and over again, in metaphor and parable, Jesus reiterated the great truth that was born in Judaism, "The earth is the Lord's and all that is in it, the world, and those who live in it ..." (Psalm 24:1). Humans are laborers with God, owning nothing, holding it a little while in trust and accounting to God for the way it is used. This is the basic principle of our Hebrew-Christian faith.

And we had better agree with that, for all the facts are with it. Dr. Ralph Sockman tells how a New York law firm was engaged to clear the title to some property in New Orleans. The New York firm, in turn, engaged a New Orleans attorney to get the data from the records. The lawyer traced it back as far as 1803, but the New York firm wrote him that he hadn't gone back far enough. In due time they received this letter: "Gentlemen: Please be advised that in the year 1803 the United States of America acquired the territory of Louisiana from the Republic of France by purchase. The Republic of France, in turn, acquired title from the Spanish crown by conquest; the Spanish crown having obtained it by virtue of the discovery of one Christopher Columbus, a Genoese sailor, who had been authorized to embark by Isabella, Queen of Spain, who obtained sanction from the Pope, the Vicar of Christ, who is the son and heir of Almighty God, who made Louisiana."

Well that goes back far enough. And behind the humor is the solid truth: "The earth is the Lord's and all that is in it ..." It belongs to God. The earth is the Lord's by right of creation, by right of maintenance through God's law, and by right of redemption through God's son who brings God's holy will into historic reality.

No one saw so deeply into, or grasped so firmly, the total meaning of the divine ownership of earth and life as did Jesus Christ in the parable of the talents. You will recall how the owner of the property gave three servants various talents: one five, another two, and the third, one. Telling them to take care of the trust to the best of their ability, he went on a far journey. While he was away the man with five talents made five, the man with two talents made two, and the man with one talent buried it in the ground. When the owner returned he rewarded the first two and condemned the third.

The parable is open to many interpretations, but only one concerns us at this point. The talents belonged ultimately to their owner all the time. He had them on call whenever he chose. He had merely loaned them to the three stewards. Whether a man got five talents or two or one, he was answerable to the one who owned them all along. The question before the stewards was not, "Who owns these talents?" The only question before them was, "To what use shall I put the talent(s) that has been entrusted to me?" Now, whether we like it or not, we are stewards before God of all we have. And the question we must ask of ourselves is not, "How little can I get by with?" but "What will I do with what has been entrusted to me?"

Dr. Luther Powell reminds us that: "We have been entrusted with the gospel of Jesus Christ and have been given the gift of eternal life, and that it is our high calling to share this gift with others. The one requirement placed on a steward is that the steward be found faithful. The ministry of Christian giving is fulfilled to the extent that a person is faithful in the stewardship of the gospel and all that is that person's to share." (Luther P. Powell, *Money and the Church*, New York, Association Press, 1962, p. 236)

No farmer ever goes out to his ten-acre field with a little five-pound sack of wheat under his arm saying, "How much can I get by with?" The farmer wants a harvest and comes saying "How much will it take?" The farmer is a co-worker with God. A steward. A dispenser of the magnificently varied grace of God. Christian stewardship is a matter of basic values. It is essential to the practice of the Christian religion and not merely an appendage. It is part of our wholeness, as those who have been entrusted with blessings beyond measure, that we care for everything that has been put into our hands in a manner which serves God's will and purpose.

Stewardship involves all of life. We are stewards of our emotions. They are the driving power of life. People are moved by feelings more than facts. We are stewards of our minds. A mind is a gift and with its power to think, reason, and decide it is the wonder of the ages. We are stewards of our hearts, for out of the heart are the issues of life. We are stewards of our wills. Someone has called our wills "the supreme implement of human achievement." All of these put together make up our total personality, of which we are stewards. Our personalities are like an empire which is given to us to subdue, discipline, and develop for the benefit of humanity and to the glory of God. We are stewards of our souls: "Bless the Lord, O my soul, and all that is within me, bless his holy name. Bless the Lord, O my soul, and do not forget all his benefits — who forgives all your iniquity, who heals all your diseases, who redeems your life from the Pit, who crowns you with steadfast love and mercy, who satisfies you with good as long as you live so that your youth is renewed like the eagle's" (Psalm 103:1-5).

And we are stewards of our possessions. All that we have and are ultimately belongs to God. We are partners with God in ministry and mission. We are called to involvement, responsible involvement:
- as we communicate to others what we believe;
- as we live out our faith and touch others by our example;
- as we minister to the needy;
- as we seek to understand the problems of those who have no spiritual resources;
- as we enlarge and enrich the program of our community and our congregation through our time and talents;
- and as we give generously and sacrificially to the total Christian enterprise through the stewardship of money.

Our mandate for mission is to the whole world, and money is an indispensable tool. We may not be able to be everywhere at once in this wide world, but part of us can still be helpfully, usefully, skillfully, and dynamically involved. What we cannot do ourselves, our money does for us. In a classic statement, Dr. Harry Emerson Fosdick says:

> *The avenues are open down which our pennies, our dollars, and our millions can walk together in an accumulating multitude to the spiritual nurture of all humankind. Each of us can take some of our nerve and sinew, reduced in wages to the form of money, and through money, which is a naturalized citizen of all lands and speaks all languages, can be at work wherever the sun shines.*

It is one of the miracles of our day that a person busy at his or her daily tasks at home can yet be doing the gospel throughout the entire world — preaching, teaching, healing in response to the Great Commission of our Lord. Apart from the church's ministry through people and their gifts, God has no other plan for the world's salvation.

The mission of the church is the mission of Christ himself, and stewardship is the channel. Praying in the Upper Room our Lord set great forces in motion for the redemption of humankind, as he blessed his disciples, present and future, for the task that was theirs: "As you have sent me into the world," he prayed, "so I have sent them into the world" (John 17:18). We are dispensers of the magnificently varied grace of God.

What we do this day, as we dedicate our pledges, is no isolated act. It has worldwide implications. We have been entrusted with a holy responsibility. We have been bought with a price. We have also been bought for a purpose: witnessing to the love and lordship of Christ's ministry in the world and to the world — beginning in our local community and reaching to the ends of the earth. It is an awesome moment as we reaffirm our partnership, in the message of the cross, with him who personally wrote that message with his very life. Our Lord stretched himself upon the cross in a sacrifice that had and has a life-changing, world-shaping influence. We are called upon to stretch our commitment as individuals and as a congregation so that momentum will continue — proclaiming the goodness of God's love through Christ for the salvation of the world, and our own as well.

Part IV

Nurturing Children And Youth

Introduction To Stewardship For Children

Until recently, stewardship in most churches was considered a predominately adult concept to be encouraged and talked about once a year. In recent years, however, many have made a concerted effort to involve all ages in coming to understand stewardship as a way of life lived in gratitude for all God has given to us.

Establishing The Stewardship Habit

This period is more often associated with preschool and younger elementary children. Children this young are great imitators. They see parents bringing their envelopes each week and are eager to bring one of their own. With very young children, we have the opportunity of encouraging a giving pattern that grows as the child also grows.

The sad truth is that the manner in which offerings are received in many church school classes is not conducive to helping children come to sense their giving as a way of thanking God. Offerings are not received in a way that says thanks or communicates gratitude. Children are very generous by nature, so we miss a great opportunity when we do not encourage giving.

Young children from the age of two or three can share in the total church budget by receiving offering envelopes that encourage regular giving. Not only does this help establish the habit of regular giving, but it encourages the child and the family, by reminding us of our gratitude, even when we are absent from the church community. They can also begin to see and understand the place and use their offering has in the church. Making an intentional effort to receive offerings in a way that makes it more than an admittance price is very important. Offerings need always be received in an attitude of thanksgiving.

A child's understanding of offerings in the church could be expanded by special times when they are reminded how offerings are used. Teachers (and parents) might continually remind children why people of God offer their gifts. You might take ten pennies and tell how they might be spent in your own church. You might sit together in church and follow the offering out some morning and let a deacon or trustee tell some of the ways the money is used to help other people.

Throughout this early childhood period, we need to be creative in our approach to stewardship in order that these very young people can begin to start stewardship habits that can grow as quickly as their young bodies and minds.

Period Of Interpretation

This period generally starts with elementary-aged children and makes use of the natural curiosity children have. Children often wonder just how their offerings are used. This is a great time to begin to expand the idea of sharing to include other people. As they begin to share their toys and enjoy being on the receiving end as well, they can come to grasp the idea of sharing our gifts with others who need a smile, a hug, some help in their yard, or financial assistance. It is an opportune time to begin telling about the work of the church in other parts of the world. It is time to share the ways their own church is involved with people or projects in other communities or countries. It is a time for the children to become involved in some form of direct outreach through some specific ministry.

Some churches have selected mission projects for children that involve other children, such as bringing baby items for layettes or taking a special offering for children whose homes have been destroyed. Some involve their children in projects making peace cranes or singing to shut-ins. There are limitless opportunities in any community for ways of involving children in real ways that lead to a deepening understanding of stewardship as a commitment to a giving way of life.

There is a special opportunity with elementary children to help them see the broad scope of the mission of the church. Most missionaries — national or international — have programs that can hook the imagination of children and help them to glimpse insights into another people or culture. As leaders and workers with children, we miss golden opportunities when we do not take advantage of any way we have of interpreting our ministries with God's people throughout the world.

It is certainly appropriate for a youth pledge program to be introduced to children by grade four at the latest. Such a program would be designed to encourage children to begin to share the money they earn by doing odd jobs or through their regular allowance received for their work in the family chores. As Christians we believe we have been called to a new way of living. Our purpose in a pledging program for elementary children is to communicate the obligations, as well as the privileges, of a Christian commitment in a way that encourages deeper understanding and growth.

Moving Towards Personal Commitment

By the time young people have entered junior high school, they have begun to identify ways of deepening their commitment by sensing their role in the stewardship of the earth, of their life, of the use of their time. They have begun internalizing the idea that they must live as good stewards of all the possessions God has given to them. Many have already become involved in activities and programs which help broaden their perspectives. They are more aware of the special seasons celebrated throughout the church year.

A pledging program which recognizes them as important members of the church community, which is intentional about the way they are included in church-wide plans and which is sincere in contacts that involve pledging, will build a foundation that informs their giving as adults.

A Summary

There is no set age when pledging is designed to become a part of a church's program. But like other educational endeavors, the earlier it is practiced, the sooner it can be incorporated in a person's value system. Whether it begins with preschool or elementary or even youth, we in the church must be intentional about including children whenever we focus on stewardship. Living a life of good stewardship involves a commitment to a way of life that reflects gratitude and thanksgiving for all God has done for us. That is our calling and that is our challenge! (From *Stewardship Through the Years*, a resource of the Presbytery of Lake Michigan, Anna Kay Baker, editor. Used by permission)

The Church School Teacher As A Stewardship Enabler

When we think of the many tasks performed by church school teachers, it is easy to see them as Bible students and leaders. That is their primary task. We see them as interpreters of mission — persons who help their students catch a vision of the far-reaching implications of the gospel message. We see them as historians as they help open the eyes of their students to the contributions of past saints (and the not so saintly) and the implications of past events in the church's life. We see them as believers who elect to share their faith with children and youth that they may come to believe.

Seldom have we looked to church school teachers as those who model stewardship. That is, seldom have they been seen as having anything much to do with stewardship until November when most churches are in the midst of their financial campaigns. Two convictions make us look closely at their role. First, stewardship involves more than finances. It is a way of life. When Christians are confronted with the message of the gospel, the real confrontation comes as they attempt to work out the way in which that good news will be reflected in the way they live. That is stewardship in the broadest terms. Who is in a better position to encourage, enable, and facilitate thoughtful responses than teachers who share their life decisions with their classes. Secondly, throughout his ministry, Jesus modeled a "still better way" for us to live, teach, and to respond. As we examine the scriptures we find Jesus in many roles challenging the people to give their gifts, their talents, and their lives to being better stewards of the skills and abilities entrusted to them by their Creator God.

Builder

As contractors begin to build new houses, their first concern is the kind of foundation upon which the house is to be built. The same is true in the building of our Christian faith. As we begin to grow in our understanding of what it means to live a faithful response to God, the first contacts we have in the church are very important. For many of us, the church school teacher is the first major contact with an adult in the covenant community. The teacher's job, then, is to help individuals come to know that they are full and valued members of that covenant community — the family of God. The first three seconds are the most important in the entire classroom experience. The way children are greeted, made to feel welcome, and encouraged to be a part of what is happening all combine to make them feel they are important. They come to know they are missed when not present. As teachers you can help children come to identify and appreciate the gifts they have which are valuable to you and the group. Encourage students to pursue their unique gifts so that in discovering them, they may fulfill the potential of their creation.

As a builder, teachers can provide many informal opportunities for students to strengthen and broaden their vision of the meaning of stewardship. The way an offering is received says something about the importance we give to the act of sharing. If the offering plate serves as an admittance to the room, students begin to sense giving as a mandatory obligation instead of a joyful response to all we have been given. There is a subtle difference in the two basic terms we tend to use for the gathering of the offerings — collection and offering. *Collection* has a connotation of something being taken from someone, while *offering* is handed over by the giver. It is preferred that we use the term *offering* to denote a gift freely given by the person. Of course, the most valuable lessons will be learned as you and your students talk about ways they have and can continue to give themselves to God. It is in sharing the struggles we experience trying to identify God's will for our life that others come to know and expect God to act in and through them as well.

Confronter

As in anything else, there are times when we settle into a routine which seems appropriate at the time, but has in reality become a rut. Paul Tournier in his book, *The Meaning of Persons*, says "Habits are like spiderwebs that soon become ropes." The challenge to us in deepening our commitment to stewardship is to continue to grow in understanding. In order to help us break through those ropes we must be confronted with new ideas, new visions, and be challenged to deepen our commitment.

Jesus, in his role as confronter, did not hesitate to ask the difficult questions. He did not hesitate to call persons to task if their world had become self-serving and self-centered. When the Rich Fool declared he would build bigger barns to hold the harvest, Jesus called him a fool, saying that those who lay up treasure for themselves are not rich toward God. When Jesus confronted Zacchaeus, he reminded him that the way to the kingdom of heaven is not through the gathering of material wealth. Through this confrontation, Jesus challenged them to seek a better way of living — a way that would satisfy the heart rather than the purse. So we as teachers must want our students to live lives filled with the riches of the spirit. To do that they must be confronted time and again as they begin to make choices that will affect the stewardship of their lives.

Challenger

When Jesus walked up to Peter and called him Rock, those who knew Peter surely must have laughed. He was as far from being a rock as anyone could have been. Yet Jesus cut through Peter's weak veneer and was able to see the potential that was in him. So it is that church school teachers are called to look into the hearts of their students and see in them the potential they either fail to see or admit to having. That puts a large responsibility on teachers as they must come to know students as individuals rather than only as a group. It means spending time with each one at some point trying to get to know his/her possibilities. It means pushing and prodding in ways that enable students to be free to test and try out new behaviors and new activities. It means providing an environment that lets students know they will be supported and nurtured in their quest.

In Romans 23 we are challenged not to think too highly of ourselves, but to look at others with sober judgment, recognizing all we are and have and will be are from God. As such, our gifts are natural treasures given to us in creation to be used for the glory of God that God might be glorified. As in the parable of the talents, those who bring the gifts are given more. As more is given, more is required in order that God might receive the praise. As teachers, we are called to challenge our students to find new ways of sharing God's creation, to expect and even demand their best, and to be examples to them of persons continuing to be on a pilgrimage of faith.

Giving Attitude

As in any other endeavor, our attitude will greatly affect and influence our students. Our attitude about the tasks we accept will speak more loudly than the words we say with our lips. The little boy who gave his loaves and fishes, and the widow who dropped her two coins in the offering, shout the joy of giving by sharing very freely the little they had in the spirit of praise for their God. Children imitate adults. When they see adults giving their time and money and skills to the glory of God they are freed to search for ways in their own young lives that they might also share.

Parents have said they see in their children a warm sense of concern for others that is often thwarted at the hands of adults. As teachers the opportunity is there to help cultivate that concern and to bring to bear witness to the fact that God is in charge of our lives. Our task is to live as faithful caretakers and stewards of that which we have been given.

Other Roles

As stewardship enablers, teachers are farmers that sow seeds that will sprout and bear fruit in some other time and place perhaps. They are called to be storytellers of the faith, telling parables and stories that illustrate the call to faithful stewardship in our lives. And finally, we are called to be interpreters of the need for financial support for the ministry and mission of the church. The role of church school teacher is more than leading a special session during the church's stewardship season. It is a continuous process of growth into a deepening commitment to live the entirety of our lives in faithful obedience to God. For many, that process will begin with you — the church school teacher. (From *Stewardship Through the Years*, a resource of Lake Michigan Presbytery, Anna Kay Baker, editor. Used by permission)

The Youth Budget

The church, along with parents, is responsible for nurturing children and youth in the meaning of stewardship. In the communicants' training especially, at least one session should be spent in providing a practical and theological basis for a commitment to church membership that is expressed materially as well as spiritually. Such a commitment needs to express itself in grateful giving both as a response to God's grace and as a vital part of Christian fellowship and growth.

Not only must class training be provided but the local church also needs to offer some kind of compatible stewardship program which will both challenge junior high and senior high youth and at the same time offer them a partnership involvement. Increasingly, the cultivation of financial support by communicant members in particular, and youth in general, is a neglected area. Obviously, this has serious future implications. Some churches have used what is known as the youth budget program in which young people establish a certain percent or amount of the total congregational budget as their responsibility. This gives a more personal identification with what is happening in the whole life of the congregation.

The program is adaptable, adjustable, and provides unlimited opportunity for creativity on the part of youth. All junior high and senior high youth are invited to make a pledge. Special pledge cards may be designed for youth use only. These cards are distributed during the church's annual stewardship by peers through personal contact or mail, which should include a letter of explanation. At the same time an interpretive and informative letter could also be sent to parents. Such a program is invaluable as a teaching and training experience. Equally important, it gives the congregation an awareness of youth interest, involvement, and participation.

Young people today are handling increasingly larger amounts of money because of better paying part-time jobs or more generous allowances. Given a chance to shape their own priorities, they are often far more visionary in their generosity than adults. Young people who are excited about stewardship will often pledge as much or more than adults who have become static in their spiritual growth and corresponding financial response. Many youth learn the discipline of both proportionate and regular giving through participating in the youth budget program. The experience trains them for the present and marks them for life.

A Youth Budget Committee may be elected or appointed by the church's Stewardship Committee or the Youth Cabinet. The committee meets in late summer or early fall to plan, set a theme, and establish a realistic budget quota. The goal that is established becomes a part of the total church budget. In other words, the youth goal may be set (by the youth) at $4,000 toward the total church goal of $400,000. And the quota should have a benevolence component which needs to be lifted up to the youth and the full congregation as well. Of the $4,000 goal, the youth may elect to use 25 percent of the total for benevolences, a three-to-one proportion. That proportion could go higher or lower according to the decision made by the Youth Budget Committee and can change yearly.

The Youth Budget Committee also plans what type of promotion and presentation will be given to church school classes and youth groups. Members of the Youth Budget Committee often write and produce their own material. In churches where the youth budget is also used in grades three through six, the committee can produce material using skits, puppets, slides, video, or other dramatic presentations. Posters by young artists are placed around the building. Initial letters of interpretation need to be drafted by the committee to be sent to all junior high and senior high youth to tell them about the youth budget, when and how pledge cards will be distributed, and inviting them to be present in the worship service on Pledge Dedication Sunday. Also, follow-up letters should be drafted inviting those who have not pledged by a certain date to return their pledge cards as soon as possible. The letter should contain a second pledge card. The whole process is not intended to put undue pressure on youth. But it is designed to indicate that stewardship is an essential ingredient of the Christian life involving the commitment of each individual.

Part V

Stewardship As Worship, Ministry, And Mission

Pledge Dedication Sunday

The Sunday that pledges are dedicated is a significant day and should be given a special name: Pledge Dedication Sunday, Consecration Sunday, Loyalty Sunday, or Stewardship Commitment Sunday. The date should be set well in advance. Through the years this can become a fixed and important event in the life of the congregation. It needs to be lifted up as a high and holy occasion so that people become increasingly sensitive to the fact that pledging is not merely a routine event but a sacred experience. "I will pay my vows to the Lord in the presence of all his people" (Psalm 116:18).

Worship for the day needs careful planning and preparation. It is an exciting and inspiring celebration as well as a meaningful and motivating experience when people present their pledges to the glory of God. Alter the service allowing for extra music and a special pledging ceremony. Devote a generous portion of the bulletin to stewardship. Emphasize the significance of pledging as an affirmation of highest praise and deepest devotion combining faith with works and believing with doing.

All choirs should be used on this Sunday. Many parents will want to hear their children sing. Massed choirs also give visibility to something the people support through their giving. Many voices add to the celebrative mood. Have a processional with banners. Select anthems carefully. Sing about the church and its world mission. Preach about the spiritual and theological implications of stewardship. Hold before the congregation their responsibility for continued personal growth through giving — "your very giving proves the reality of your faith" (2 Corinthians 9:13 J. B. Phillips).

Immediately after the sermon, invite the congregation to worship through pledging. This can take two forms: members may be invited to come forward to the communion table and place their pledges in containers on the table or in front of the table. This affirms the sacramental nature of the pledge which in essence is an outward act with an inner meaning. This can be a very moving personal experience. Or, the ushers can use the offering plates to collect the pledges of the people using the same procedure that is used in taking the offering. However, the offering should not be received at that time, only pledges. The offering should be received at another place in the service.

When the sermon is finished the pastor says with confidence and enthusiasm:

1. (Pledge Sunday) is our opportunity to worship through pledging.
2. What First Church does in 2000 here at home, in this community, in the United States, and its possessions, and throughout the world, depends on what our congregation does today.
3. Pledge cards are in the pew racks for those who may have misplaced theirs.
4. Friends of First Church (non-members) may also make a pledge and participate in the on-going program and mission of this congregation.
5. Before performing the act of loyalty, let us read together the Prayer of Consecration in your bulletin.

    O God, our gracious and generous creator, we gratefully acknowledge your ownership and recognize our stewardship. All we have is a trust from you. We thank you that through Christ's love, we have learned the relationship between giving and living. Teach us to give as loyal partners with him. We would pledge to you an honorable share of our income. May our pledges express our genuine, sincere faith and true loyalty. Use us and our offerings to extend the worldwide kingdom of him who loved us and gave himself for us. In his name we pray and pledge. Amen.

6. At this time we invite you to come forward and place your pledges in the receptacles in front of the communion table. Or, I shall now ask the ushers to come forward and wait on you, as you give your pledge to your church, and with it yourself, your soul and body, in renewed consecration to Christ's cause.

At this point the choir may sing an anthem. Or appropriate music may be played while the people are coming forward with their pledges or while the ushers are collecting the pledges in offering plates. When completed the congregation rises and sings the Doxology and a Prayer of Dedication is said in unison:

> Almighty God, giver of every good and perfect gift, who has shown us that it is more blessed to give than to receive, we dedicate these pledges to the service of your church, humbly praying that all our gifts and energies may be used in the extension of your kingdom here on earth. Accept these pledges, we pray; multiply them in your service and then transform them into loving deeds of grace and mercy, given in Christ's name and to the everlasting glory of your name — for the sake of Jesus Christ. Amen.

Immediately following the prayer, the organ begins the closing hymn: "All Hail the Power of Jesus' Name." In triumphant song this meaningful service is brought to a stirring climax. Planning, prayer, hard work, and thoughtful preparation all culminate in a moving spiritual experience. As the celebrative tradition continues to gain momentum, attendance likewise grows so that the entire church family sees it as an occasion of highest magnitude, which in actuality it really is.

Now Thank We All Our God

For over 300 years one of the favorite Thanksgiving hymns has been Martin Rinkart's "Now Thank We All Our God," the first line of which reads: "Now thank we all our God, with heart and hands and voices ..." Written at the end of the Thirty Years War for the people of his native Saxony, it comes out of a background of personal suffering, tragedy, and horrible privation. With it, he called the people of his parish and community to renewal and rebuilding, thanking God that their lives had been spared. True gratitude, as the hymn expresses, begins with an inner state of appreciation which evidences itself through deeds and words. November is the time of year when we give special thanks to God for our abundant blessings as individuals, as Christians, and as a nation. Out of the background of our abundance we have an opportunity to profess and proclaim our inner awareness.

Pledge Dedication Sunday is the day when love and loyalty climax in a Service of Dedication. It is a time when hands with a capacity to work and earn, write the amount of self-involvement as a pledge and then the card is "handed in" on the offering plate. This is not some mechanical fund-raising act. It is a sacramental experience by which inner gratitude is tangibly demonstrated. On Thanksgiving Day we gather in the sanctuary to bless God for all our gifts through songs and prayers of praise. Pledge Dedication Sunday and Thanksgiving Day are two holy occasions when we acknowledge "with heart and hands and voices" our gratitude, God's ownership, humanity's indebtedness, and our response to God's love expressed in Christ our Lord.

Your Mission Through Your Pledge

The story is told of the minister whose church served a large rural parish in a rich farming section of our country. One day while driving down a country lane, he passed a parishioner's farm. It was a fine farm, with lush crops, well-painted barns and houses, and was obviously well-tended. Struck by the beauty of the pastoral scene, the minister stopped his car and gazed with admiration. The farmer recognized his pastor, stopped his tractor, and came to exchange across-the-fence pleasantries.

In the course of the conversation, the minister learned that only 25 years earlier the entire farm was woodland and had been cleared for crops by the parishioner and his family. "What a wondrous work the Lord has done here," exclaimed the minister. "Yep," said the farmer, taking a firmer grip on the straw he was chewing, "but you know, Parson, this farm is really a partnership — the Lord and me. Like you say on Sunday, God brings the rain and sun and makes things grow. I manage the place for God, and that's important too, because you should have seen the place before I bought it, and the Lord was in charge."

So it is with the church. We, too, are partners with the Lord. God provides the "fields white with harvest: the young to be given Christian nurture, the sick to be consoled and supported, the heavy-hearted to be comforted, the marriage to be sanctified, the troubled to be counseled, the community to be challenged, the churchless to be brought to God, and the good news brought to the ends of the earth."

God sets us in the midst of the world, in a particular place, to minister to the world-at-large. Through education, medicine, evangelism, agricultural aids, and other creative services, God permits the church and its mission to be a channel of Christ's love and hope to a world waiting for the light of the world. We must provide the means to meet the needs — "to get in the harvest." We have a vital part in the partnership.

What does this have to do with stewardship? Webster defines a steward as: "a person put in charge of the affairs of a large household or estate...." So, like the farmer, we must have a program which will enable our partnership to do what God has called us to do as individuals and as a congregation. God will give the vision, the courage, and the strength. We must supply the time, the talent, and the treasure. If each member will take one step up in the year to come, with God's blessing, the church can move ten paces forward.

Worshiping God

The modern word "worship" derives from one of those beautiful old Anglo-Saxon roots: *woerthscipe*, which means "worthiness," "repute," or "respect." Originally, the word referred to a person of honor, as when a citizen referred to the king as "your worship."

There are many ways to worship the Most Worthy. We can fall to our knees. We can pray. We can praise. We can sing. We can conduct our daily lives with such honor and beauty that the One we serve is proud to call us citizens of the Kingdom. But there is nothing more honoring, honorable, and worshipful than in putting our money where are mouths are — in church.

In some ways, our gift to the church is the highest and most concrete act of worship we perform, simply because it is the most difficult; it requires us to sacrifice the work of our hands, the fruit of our labors, a good portion of the legal tender with which we might otherwise have purchased many of the good things of life. The way we spend our money is the most eloquent testimony to what we consider worthy and honorable.

When you stop to think about all that God has given — this shining planet, friends to cherish, a bountiful board, a son at Calvary — God doesn't ask for much, only a small portion — an hour a week in praise, a couple more in service to church and community, small daily acts of mercy and justice. You get to keep at least ninety percent of your hours and dollars. That's not a bad deal, as deals go. Won't you respond extravagantly to God's extravagance? (William A. Evertsberg, "Worshipping God," CHIMES, newsletter of Westminster Church of Grand Rapids, November, 1995)

Putting Faith Into Practice

There is an old story of a doctor in a French village who was about to retire. He had been on call day and night; the people could not afford to pay him much, but that had made no difference. He cared for them as he was able.

As the day of retirement approached the people wished to make a concrete expression of their gratitude and affection. It was proposed that on a given day, since they had so little money to give, they bring a pitcher of wine from their own cellars and pour it into a large barrel placed in the village square, which in turn would be presented to the doctor, as an expression of their affection and gratitude.

The day arrived and all day long the people poured their offerings into the barrel. The evening came and the barrel was taken to the doctor's humble residence and presented, with all the inevitable speeches. The presentation over, the people went back to their homes and the doctor was left with the memory of their love.

He went to the barrel and drew off a bit of wine, then went into the house and sat comfortably by the fire to enjoy it. The first sip was a shock. It tasted like water. He sipped again. It was water! He went back to the barrel and drew off more, thinking there must have been some queer mistake. But no, the barrel was filled with water.

He called the Mayor and the Mayor called the Assemblymen and there were hurried consultations. Then the truth was revealed. Everyone in the town had reasoned: "My little pitcher of wine won't be missed. I have so little for myself. The others will take care of it. The little water I substituted will not be noticed."

It is a tragic story. It may have never happened; but it is the kind of thing that can and does happen when people rationalize their responsibility. It is not hard to do in light of the above story. "I have so little for myself. What I have to offer won't be missed. The others will take care of it." Yet it can even happen with Christians who say: "I have so little, my pledge will never be missed.

My small increase will not be important. Let the others take care of it."

On the other hand, when you give money to the church, you return part of yourself to Christ, as an expression of your faith and commitment, to be used for his work on earth. You are where your money goes. You have a partnership in the local ministry of your church, and in the various governing bodies with which your church is connected and countless other avenues through which Christ's mission is accomplished.

Putting your pledge card (hopefully with an increase) and then your money in the offering plate is no isolated act. It has universal implications.

Mission – What It Is

The Christian mission is one:
   It is not faith or works but both.
   It is not mission at home or mission around the world but both.
   It is not giving or receiving but both.
   It is not growing in personal piety or empowering the powerless but both.
   The Christian is sent to all others at all times and in all places, to declare by word and action the life-giving Good News of the Risen Christ!

The Christian mission is eternal:
   Our Lord's command to go into all the world overarches all of time, from the Roman empire days to the new millennium to all the tomorrows to come. Yesterday's mission barrel, today's ecumenical partnerships, tomorrow's as yet unformed designs — all are Christian mission, expressions of the infinite love of God for all God's children. *God has the keenest and freshest memory of the forgotten!*

The Christian mission is unique:
   Many people offer food to the hungry.
   Many agencies offer economic, medical, and educational help.
   Many faiths offer partial remedies for life's incurable ills.
   Many creeds offer a measure of understanding of the mysteries of life and death.

But only the gospel of Christ offers all of these:
   Steadfastness in the face of tragedy and oppression;
   Humility stronger than any earthly power;
   A loving person-to-person bond that transcends time and space;
   The freedom to celebrate life, whatever one's condition;
   An inexhaustible joy which grows in those who share it;
   Never-failing forgiveness of sins;
   A cross that speaks of the ultimacy of God's love and grace;

A faith that is stronger than death and assurance of victory at the last;
A hope that shall endless be.

God intends that each Christian shall offer one's brother or sister more than an ecclesiastical pattern; one must offer a personal savior. **If the committed Christian does not offer all of these, no one else will, because no one else can.**

Your Church Involves You

Your church
- Involves you in the community that remembers and recognizes Jesus Christ
- Welcomes you at birth and baptizes you in the Christian faith
- Stimulates spiritual maturity through worship and study
- Provides principles to guide you in daily living
- Stands ready to counsel with you in time of need
- Gives you a context in which to express thanks for what you have received
- Points to the deeper meaning of marriage and family life
- Hears your call in times of sickness and trouble
- Offers you a supportive fellowship in the name of Christ
- Proclaims to you God's forgiveness of sins
- Provides a means for alleviating society's ills and human needs
- Remembers and appreciates you in your later years
- Stands with you in times of sorrow and death
- Comforts you with the message of Christian hope
- Gives you a part in God's work in God's world
- Serves as a channel for translating faith into action

In the act of worship, when you give, this becomes the personal expression of your love, concern, and gratitude, which is translated into action and service by those who represent you here and throughout the world. *You are involved!*

We are called upon to give as God has given to us. This is the standard the Bible teaches: planned, purposeful, and proportionate giving. For faithful Christians there can be no other way. Partnership is not a matter of occasional impulse or fortuitous surplus, but a constancy in response to God's constancy.

Dollar for dollar, no other institution that exists today gives greater service to humanity than the (your) church. (Bishop James L. Duncan)

A Poem For Pledge Dedication Sunday

Jericho Road Again

I've just gone down to Jericho again —
I've gone a thousand times before; but each time in the past,
With book in hand and eyes on printed page,
I failed to see the man.
This time, I left the book at home — and walked the road alone —
I SAW PEOPLE ALL AROUND.
Some of their wounds were old — and some were new —
And compassion came rising in my heart —
I could not pass them by.
The Jericho Road is any street — and every road
Where we see — and hear — and feel —
AND HELP!
We become aware of our identity with others —
In the bundle of life.
The word neighbor comes alive for us.
GOOD SAMARITAN BECOMES OUR NAME!
Wherever compassion gets the best of us —
Wherever our hearts and hands and money—
Go out recklessly — gladly — joyously and generously —
and in God's name and for Christ's sake —
THAT IS OUR JERICHO ROAD!

Truly I tell you, just as you did it to one of the least of these who are members of my family, you did it to me. (Matthew 25:40b)

A Hymn For Pledge Dedication Sunday

As Those Of Old Their First Fruits Brought

As those of old their first fruits brought
Of vineyard flock and field
To God the giver of all good,
The source of bounteous yield,
So we today our first fruits bring,
The wealth of this good land:
Of farm and market, shop and home,
Of mind and heart and hand.

A world in need now summons us
To labor, love and give.
To make our life an offering
To God that all may live.
The church of Christ is calling us
To make the dream come true:
A world redeemed by Christ-like love,
All life in Christ made new.

With gratitude and humble trust
We bring our best to You,
Not just to serve Your cause, but share
Your love with neighbors too.
O God who gave Yourself to us
In Jesus Christ Your Son,
Help us to give ourselves each day
Until life's work is done.

AS THOSE OF OLD THEIR FIRST FRUITS BROUGHT
Text: Frank Von Christierson
Text ©
1961. Renewed 1989 The Hymn Society. Admin. By Hope Publishing Co., Carol Stream, IL 60188. All rights reserved. Used by permission. Contact Hope Publishing Company for permission to reprint, 800-323-1049

Part VI

Bequests As Blessings

The Stewardship Of Bequests

A well-to-do member and Trustee of a congregation once said at a regular meeting of the Board of Trustees: "I'm not going to leave one cent of my money to this church. Do you know why? Because I don't trust you with my money."

He said it with a twinkle in his eye. But he caught the attention of the Board. He was advocating an Endowment Trust with an established present and future policy of applied stewardship regarding bequests. He made the following points:
- The membership of the Board changes regularly due to rotation and the action of one Board can be set aside by a new Board.
- Without established guidelines and a proper legal instrument, gifts and bequests could be diverted to operational needs or used in a manner incompatible with the general intent of the donor.
- Donors want to be assured that their continuing Christian influence is both protected and perpetuated.
- The "larger church," although implicit in the donor's decision to give to the local church, can be ignored by rationalizing the urgency of home needs.
- Every church should have a written policy stating that a proportion of all undesignated bequests be used for benevolent/mission purposes.

Within six months the Board of Trustees recommended to the congregation an Endowment Trust plan that included a tithe of all unrestricted bequests for mission purposes as well as a practical program for the use of interest while keeping the corpus intact. From time to time in the previous eighty-year history of that congregation bequests had been given and then used for immediate operating needs. Nothing existed to give evidence, on the part of the previous donors, of their continuing Christian influence. After five years of an approved legal and publicized Endowment Fund, many gifts and bequests were given to that church by numerous donors who felt confident about the stewardship of their love and commitment expressed through a financial gift.

Suggestions Regarding The Stewardship Of Bequests
- Every congregation, regardless of size, should establish an Endowment Trust.
- Every congregation should establish a formula for all unrestricted bequests so that mission giving receives a certain percent of the total amount. Some churches tithe all undesignated bequests by giving ten percent of the total amount to benevolences. Others use a "two-to-one" formula, giving one-third for mission. And still others divide undesignated bequests in half: fifty percent for benevolences and fifty percent to be placed in trust. Such a formula needs to be approved by the governing body and adopted by the congregation as church policy.
- Every congregation should establish a policy indicating that the benevolence percentage from an unrestricted bequest will be used as a plus gift *over and above* that which is contributed by the congregation for the regular mission/benevolence budget of the church.
- In addition — every congregation should formulate a policy of percentage distribution of that portion of the bequest to be used for benevolences which includes: local needs, special needs, and denominational mission. Since the bequest was made to a church affiliated with a denomination it should be assumed, unless otherwise indicated by the donor, that part of the gift should be used for denominational mission purposes.
- Every governing body should publicize in writing the benevolent percent of unrestricted bequests to provide a clear example of the church's stewardship commitment.
- Every governing body should publicize the purpose of the Endowment Trust, the kind of gifts that can be given (bequests, memorials, special gifts), the projected use of interest income, the management of capital, and any other

information which expresses the continuing Christian influence and expression that such a plan provides.
- Every governing body should publicize the various ways of participating in the Endowment Trust: outright gift of cash or securities, outright gift of real estate, outright gift in kind, gift of a remainder interest in a residence or farm, gift through unitrust, gift through annuity trust, life insurance gifts.
- Every governing body should establish a regular program emphasizing the importance of making a will and encouraging members to include their church and denomination in the will.

Summary

"Endowments can be thoroughly Christian. It is not a question of having an endowment. Rather, it is a question of how we use it. Like money, there is nothing wrong with endowments themselves. The only time endowments 'kill a church' is when the leadership of the church fails to interpret the positive function and usefulness of the endowment. The pitfalls of endowments can and have been avoided. The benefits of endowments have been demonstrated again and again as there is careful planning and wise leadership with a deep sense of responsibility as Christian stewards." ("Endowments: A Biblical Base," monograph by Aaron E. Gast)

Christian Wills

Touching The Future

Every person has the duty of deciding who is to receive his or her estate after death, no matter how small or how large the estate. Every person who has dependents has an additional obligation of providing for them in a will or trust. Every Christian has a stewardship opportunity by providing for the continuing work of Christ a portion of the goods that have been accumulated in a lifetime. Planning for the future is one responsibility of our stewardship, individually and institutionally.

Dr. John W. Stewart, former pastor of Westminster Presbyterian Church of Grand Rapids, once told a memorable story that he heard about planning at Oxford University in England.

> *In the main building of New College, Oxford, an engineer discovered that the oak beams overhead were full of beetles. The college Council's concern was heightened because of the scarcity of giant trees available for such beams. One Junior Fellow suggested that there might be such oak trees on some of the University's vast properties. So they called the College's Forester. The man responded wryly. "Well, sirs, we were wonderin' when you'd be askin'."*
>
> *Upon further inquiry it was discovered that when the College was founded in the late sixteenth century, a grove of oaks had been planted to replace the beams in the main hall, should they become beetly. The instructions were handed down from one Forester to the next for 400 years. "You don't cut them oaks. Them's for the College Hall."*

Now that's foresight!

Every church and governing body should provide a means for persons to make lasting gifts which, in turn, would make available a source of funds for additional mission outreach, capital improvements, and other special projects not ordinarily included in the regular operating budget. An Endowment Trust Fund is an important stewardship tool in assisting a congregation or governing body to do more and serve more effectively in the future.

Officers of the funds can have an effective role in nurturing church members as Christian stewards with concern for both the support of current and future needs of the church. They can offer their availability to counsel about estate planning and provide workshops, seminars, and church school classes which point up the importance of making a will and ways in which bequests to the church provide personal spiritual enrichment and well as effective tools for enlarging and enhancing the mission of the church. Publicity regarding the fund can also stimulate members to think about a will as a living legacy and a significant part of their stewardship. An informational brochure should be developed listing traditional ways of participation: gifts, life insurance, real estate, memorials, unitrusts, life income plans, and so on. These brochures should be mailed to the entire congregation from time to time, be included in new member training packets, and placed on the church literature table.

A bequest is entirely from capital.
It is entirely future-oriented.
It is to the everlasting church.
Ashley Hale

Mission Through Lending

The concept of Mission Through Lending simply means that a church leaves some of its investments available for loan purposes to assist other congregations. Such a policy can be most helpful in giving needed assistance to another church and in the process help that church fulfill its mission. Money can be loaned at a rate set below the prime interest rate and thus well below the rate of interest charged on commercial loans, but still quite comparable to the rate of interest being earned on its other investments.

Mission Through Lending has been part of the ministry of First Presbyterian Church in Battle Creek for over twenty years. In illustrating this concept I have asked the Reverend Dr. David Robertson, former pastor of First Presbyterian Church, to tell something about the way it has operated in that church and how the plan came into being.

What Good A Talent (Or Five Or Ten) Can Do

It came out of need. And the old saying tells us it often does. Necessity is the mother of invention.

A church was in need. It was facing a building campaign and the costs of borrowing. A member of that church knew that a sister church, in the connectional system, was blessed with an endowment trust made possible through the legacy of a thoughtful and perceptive parishioner. And so the member followed a good biblical principle: "You have not, because you ask not." He asked. He importuned the neighboring church to consider loaning some of the money it had in the bank to a sister church.

That need, and the willingness of the church member to ask for help, led to a new concept of mission and witness for the church that was asked. Such a plan and policy could become a practice for all churches blessed with the generosity of parishioners who graciously provide for a continuing Christian witness through a bequest to their church. And that particular plan could be called Mission Through Lending.

In the case of the two churches mentioned above, the requesting church was loaned a portion of the money it needed from commercial banks at prevailing interest rates. It received some money from its denomination at a very low interest. And it received a substantial loan from its sister church. The money received was loaned at a rate of interest that was fair to the lending church in keeping faith with its members and mission, but was also fair and extremely helpful to the borrowing church which had no other source of funds. And the rate of interest was substantially lower than the banks could charge. The church that borrowed not only saved money but was greatly encouraged by the commitment of its sister church. In part, because of the financial help, the church that borrowed was subsequently able to double its mission giving in a period of five years. Mission Through Lending offers a co-partnership in the common cause of Christ.

What began as a direct response to a specific request grew into a policy of Mission Through Lending that has been helpful to a number of churches. The borrowing church is benefitted because it is dealing with a Christian neighbor. It also has increased an understanding of, and appreciation for, the connectional system or ecumenical relationships. And it is encouraged and supported in its own efforts to grow, as well as receiving a beneficial financial arrangement.

The lending church is benefitted because it becomes a further partner in Christian work. It acts as a good neighbor. It uses its "talents" wisely and well and shows a good return for the work of Christ. It aids and strengthens the work of Christ done by other Christians in a supportive relationship. And it sees itself investing in Christian ministry and participating in discipleship.

This wider fellowship helps create an atmosphere of trust and confidence that should make the policy of Mission Through Lending by a local church very attractive. For this is a way of acting out the biblical mandate to be part of the body of Christ and to use its "talents" in the wisest and most productive ways.

As the pastor of a church that has benefitted from this policy, I commend it to others as a unique Christian venture!

Sample Trust Agreement

Endowment Fund Of The
First United Church Of Stewardstowne

This Endowment Fund is created this _____ day of _____, 2001, by the governing body of Stewardstowne Church, a (*State*) ecclesiastical corporation ("the Church") with its principal officers at 111 Jones Rd., Jonesville, (*State 77777*).

1. Fund Purpose. This Trust is created for the purpose of providing an additional vehicle by which members of the church may with their lifetime gifts, memorials, and testamentary bequests contribute to the missions and ministries of the church, locally and globally, and to assist in the capital improvements of church-owned facilities.

The principle of such Fund shall be held in perpetuity, and only the income is to be spent. It serves as a vehicle to assist and encourage individuals to make gifts that will last far into the future. It seeks to attract and manage financial resources in a way that will make possible opportunities for ministry beyond the regular operating budget.

2. Fund Administration. The Endowment Fund will be administered by a committee of three (3) Trustees appointed by the Governing Body. Initially, the Governing Body will appoint one (1) Trustee for a one-year term, one (1) Trustee for a two-year term, and one (1) Trustee for a three-year term. Thereafter, each appointment will be for a three-year term. Any vacancy created by an unexpired term of a Trustee may be filled by action of the Governing Body. At least one (1) Trustee shall be a current member of the Governing Body. The senior pastor of the church will be an ex-officio non-voting member of the Endowment Fund Committee. The chairperson will be appointed annually by the Governing Body and Trustees may be appointed to successive terms.

The Trustees shall meet at least twice annually or upon the request of the chairperson. Two Trustees shall constitute a quorum. There must be a quorum present for the approval of any transaction.

The duties of the Trustees include managing the Fund's assets in accordance with their fiduciary responsibility and the guidelines established by (the constitution of the particular denomination, if any); apprise the congregation and friends of the church of the Fund's purpose and existence; encourage gifts, memorials, and bequests to the Fund; and advise the Governing Body and congregation of the receipt of assets and the distribution of income.

3. Liability Of Trustees. The Trustees of the Endowment Fund shall serve without bond or other security and shall be chargeable only with the exercise of good faith in carrying out the provisions, purpose, and intent of the Endowment Fund and its administration. The Trustees in the absence of bad faith, shall not be responsible or accountable for errors in judgment.

4. Division of Assets. The assets of the Endowment Fund shall be divided as follows:
- (a) "Unrestricted Funds." These shall be funds which have been transferred to the Endowment Fund free of restrictions save those imposed by this instrument.
- (b) "Restricted Funds." These shall be funds which have been transferred to the Endowment Fund subject to the restrictions imposed thereon by the donor or donors and accepted by the Governing Body of the church.

The Trustees shall be empowered to hold unrestricted and restricted funds in separate accounts.

5. Accounting By Trustees. The trustees shall render an accounting in the form of a written report to the Governing Body semiannually. An annual accounting shall also be prepared and distributed to the Governing Body and be made available to the congregation. The financial records of the Trust shall undergo an independent audit in a manner deemed appropriate by the Governing Body.

6. Segregation Of Accounts. Funds received by the Trustees will be placed in the following accounts:
  (a) "Endowment Account" — a permanent and perpetual fund. Funds in this account shall be invested and the principal shall not be expended. Interest from undesignated funds will be transferred to the Revolving Account.
  (b) "Revolving Account" — an operational account to which interest from unrestricted funds shall be transferred. Interest and principal from restricted funds may also be transferred to this account.

7. Distribution Of Income. Ten percent of all interest accumulated from the "Unrestricted Funds" shall be used for benevolent (mission) purposes subject to Mission Committee and Trustee recommendation and Governing Body approval. Ninety percent of all interest accumulated from "Unrestricted Funds" shall be used for capital improvements, building maintenance, debt reduction, or property acquisition. Interest shall not be allowed to accumulate. "Restricted Funds" shall be expended only pursuant to the restrictions imposed upon such funds.

8. Management Of Assets. The Trustees shall manage the assets of the Endowment Fund and shall carry it out with care for mission responsibility. They shall ordinarily invest the assets in such ways that are lawful in the (particular State) that will provide prudent security for the principal and receive maximum feasible return. Some liquidity of assets is desirable.

The Trustees may arrange for an appropriate repository for securities or other instruments, and may seek and use such professional assistance as they deem necessary. Expenses for such arrangements and/or assistance may be paid out of the income of the Endowment Fund. The Fund may be placed with (name of denominational resource, if available) for investment.

9. Amendment. This document may be amended from time to time as to procedural provisions by majority vote of the totally elected Governing Body provided that written notice of such amendment has been given to each member of the Governing Body thirty days prior to such vote. In case of extreme emergency the principal of the Unrestricted Funds may be invaded by majority vote of the total elected Governing Body, recommending such action to the congregation, provided that written notice of such amendment has been given to each member of the Governing Body thirty (30) days prior to such vote. Subsequently, a majority of the congregation must concur with the Governing Body recommendation at a duly called special meeting of the congregation.

10. Miscellaneous Provisions.
 (a) Upon approval by the Governing Body of the church this Declaration shall become fully binding upon the Church, and all parts of the Fund shall be construed as contractual and not a mere recital.
 (b) A copy of this Declaration, with the dates of its adoption and approval duly certified by an executive officer of the church, shall be kept on file in the office of the church and be open to inspection by the church members during business hours.

* * * * *

The foregoing document is hereby approved and ratified by the Governing Body of the Stewardstowne Church of (*City and State*) this _____ day of _____, 2001.

_____
Official signature

Part VII

Inspirational, Informational, And Illustrative Material

Some Titanic Thoughts On Small Thinking

Dear Friends in First Church:

Everything about us says, "think big." We live in an impressive age. Our accomplishments are vast in every area of achievement. But, by the same token, our problems are of momentous proportions. Sometimes it seems that one cancels out the other and we are merely surrounded by a kind of impartial vastness. What we are, and can do as individuals, often seems trivial, insignificant, and of minimal value.

Perhaps we take the wrong approach. Rather than thinking big, dreaming the impossible dream, and talking in "out of sight" superlatives, we need to "think small." It's a law of life that small thinking is the first step toward the realization of larger dreams. If we think small enough, perhaps there is something each of us can more realistically do to "help heal the open sore of the world."

Thinking small may mean that a person decides to increase his or her giving by one-quarter or one-half percent of total income. Or small thinking may cause one to say, "I can't give a tithe just yet, but I'd like to. So this year I'll take a step up by giving an increase of one percent of total income." Ten small thoughts like that and the person is a tither. It may take ten years — but God is patient and understanding. Few people become tithers overnight. (*A pastor or a lay person may use this illustration and then add a personal note at this point.* I've tithed for over twenty years now, but it took five years to get started. After that it was easy. And a joy. Now I'm working toward new goals.)

Thinking small has many ramifications. It means the impossible dream can become an honest reality when we go at it one small step at a time. So this year we are challenged to think small. It's amazing what happens when we put our small thoughts and acts together. Out of such thoughts and actions the multitudes are fed.

That's what happened with this lad who brought his loaves and fishes to Jesus in order to help feed the 5,000. He could have been intimidated by the mass of people and frozen by inaction. But he thought small. It was almost humorous. "Here's my little lunch, Lord, if it will help." Jesus didn't laugh at that kind of thinking or that kind of action. It was such a small and simple gesture. But with God's blessing he fed a multitude — and taught an elemental lesson in higher mathematics.

Strange as it may seem, that's what we are called upon to do — to feed multitudes by thinking small. We ought not to try it though, unless we're prepared for big surprises. This could be the most fantastic year we have ever had in First Church, simply because enough people thought small. Now that's a challenge!

To Be Spiritually Fit

To be spiritually fit, a Christian will
>*worship,*
>*learn,*
>*serve,*
>and *share.*

In worshiping — we praise God and face the unanswerables of human existence.

In learning — we participate in an open universe where God continues to speak.

In serving — we identify with Christ in his suffering and incarnation.

In sharing — we strengthen one another, find our own identity, and express our faith.

>To be an enabler, a church will offer us creative resources in worshiping, learning, serving, and sharing. And First Church does just that through ...
>**a program of education**
>**a program of missions**
>**a program of music and worship**
>**a program of pastoral care**
>**a program of recreation and weekday activity**
>(*list others*)

Each week over _____ people enter the doors of First Ecumenical Church.

We minister in the name of Christ through our stewardship of time, talents, and treasure.

Your decision —

The proportion you decide upon is an expression of your faith — the evidence of your involvement — the expression of your love!
>**We give to God**
>>THROUGH
>>>**the Budget of First Church**
>
>*Think positively — think percentages!*

God, Where Are You?

In this world of
- War
- Addiction
- Revolution
- Hunger
- Catastrophe
- Terrorism
- Brutality
- Anger

I searched for you
- in books
- in school
- in church
- in work
- in government
- in leisure
- in possessions
- in therapy

Then — I
- gave my time
- gave my talent
- gave my energy
- gave my commitment
- gave my love
- gave my strength
- gave my skills
- gave my self — gave myself to others.

And I found you
> in my giving
> by my giving
> through my giving

In all those people with whom I shared myself.
Seek and you will know that:
> *To give is to find!*

Make Mine The Same

Often in a social situation when people may be ordering in a restaurant or a hostess is asking about the type of refreshment people may desire, one person may suggest a preference and several others will respond by saying, "Make mine the same." Many times people in the group will joke (or be serious), saying we all share the same good taste. At the same time it provides an easy solution for the waiter or the hostess since it is always much easier to prepare several of the same items. No problem. Sameness has some advantages.

However, sameness has some disadvantages as well. This is particularly evident during the stewardship season when members are invited to consider making a new pledge for the forthcoming year. When contacted some will say, "I'll give the same as last year," or in essence the response is, "Make mine the same." They are continuing a pledge and obviously there is merit in that. The same pledge for a new year.

However, it is not the same pledge for a new year. In a sense that pledge will be *less* than last year. That's right. Less! Because costs will be greater. Reliable estimates show that the cost of living index rises each year. Some years there is a very modest increase and other years it may be more significant. But there is an increase each year. When one gives the same as last year, one is actually giving the church less support than in the previous year. If a pledge has remained the same for several years, that may add up to a significant decrease. Remaining the same for a new year, depending on the size of the pledge, may mean an equivalent decrease of $50, $75, or $100 for one pledge unit. That is a fairly modest amount in today's economy. But if 100 other people also say, "Make mine the same," that can have a significant influence on the church's ability to minister and be in mission.

It is easy to fall into the habit of static giving. "Make mine the same" is a much more comfortable response and often an easy way "to take care of the matter and get on to other things." However, spiritual growth is marked by financial growth as well. The two are inseparable. And that is evidenced by a conscious personal commitment to increase one's giving to the church year by year. Obviously not everyone can do that, even though it is in one's heart to do so. But most can give some kind of a proportionate increase each year. And in so doing they continue on a pilgrimage toward their full potential as Christian stewards.

Keeping The Pledge Covenant

As one thinks about pledging, it is important to remember that we all pledge. We do this through mortgages, time payments, regular utility bills, and so on. Life is full of pledges. The question therefore is not about a decision to pledge, but whether or not we will pledge to the church. A pledge to the church is a covenant: not a legal document in the secular sense, but a statement of one's intention.

In the secular world, if a pledge is not fulfilled, one may lose services, money, or possessions. That doesn't happen with a church pledge. If it is not fulfilled, the pledger loses nothing. But God does. The local church does. The neighborhood, presbytery, synod, and worldwide ministry of the General Assembly does. God's work in the world is dependent on individual Christians and what they do with what God has given them.

A church pledge is a personal and sacred commitment. In actuality it involves more than our intention to support God's work in the world. It is an expression of one's integrity as a Christian. That little pledge card, once signed, becomes a holy document. It is a demonstration of our faith, a declaration of our loyalty, and an affirmation of our priorities.

As the year ends, let us make every effort so that our intention becomes reality. (There are extraordinary times when one's best laid plans take an unforeseen turn. An informative note or telephone call to the church will bring assurance of understanding and subsequent peace of mind.)

Compassion Fatigue

We live in a day when all media constantly bombard the emotions with every imaginable horror. The staccato voice of radio brings word of calamity and tragedy far and near. The all-seeing eye of television penetrates the most remote points of the map and catches in unrelenting honesty the agony of faces, bodies, wreckage, ravage, and vivid red of flowing blood. Computer screens can do the same. Haunting songs and harshly realistic newsprint massages the imagination.

It is no wonder that individuals seem to reach a saturation point, an emotional limit where one seems to be totally immersed and heavy laden with the feeling of "What's the use? What good can my little concern be in the face of such monstrous calamity and gnawing need?"

Furthermore, as "the more fortunate" live in a world that constantly strives for cushion and comfort, it becomes increasingly difficult to project ourselves out of cozy confines into the raw and the wretched. We almost deliberately want to shut out the sights, sounds, and ugly needs that clamor for attention, amelioration, and action.

Consciously, we build barriers higher and higher, seeking for a studied detachment that will remain both objective about such things, yet somewhat responsive. It sometimes takes more understanding, effort, and empathy than we want to give it. Callousness comes easy. It seems there is never any end to well-doing.

The Kerner Report, written over a quarter of a century ago (an evaluative study of social needs in America), has a troubling sentence which continues to haunt me: "A nation conditioned by affluence might possibly be suffering from compassion fatigue, the peril of narrowing our field of vision to leave out the unpleasant view of life disfigured by sorrow and suffering, pain and poverty, hunger and harassment." The sentence chronicles what to me seems a chronic condition. The point is that increasingly our responses to special needs are routine. People do respond, and respond regularly. But their responses are not in proportion to their affluence.

In 1974 noted sociologist Roger Shinn, writing in *A. D. Magazine* (a publication of the United Presbyterian Church), called for an understanding of what small units of society can do in the midst of mounting needs. He urges individuals to move from careless extravagance to a new asceticism. His message is equally timely for today.

He says: "Individuals often feel helpless in the face of global problems. But individuals and churches can do something. At a minimum we can all undertake some symbolic acts of restraint. These acts will not transform the world. But they will raise our own consciousness and contribute to raising the social consciousness of the world's needs. Furthermore, if we contribute the cash savings from such acts to the direct relief of hunger or to united efforts to meet human needs, we make a real difference. In that way we can use mammon to serve God."

Those who are fortunate enough to be affluent, from time to time need to be reminded that people are blessed, not merely for themselves, but to equip them for greater service to God and humanity. The burden goes with the blessing. We can become increasingly a leavening influence in the world — working for peace and justice — raising standards of living for all people — overcoming poverty and hunger.

Each of us in our abundance can help make a difference in the world by the decisions we make each day on
- what we eat,
- what we throw away,
- how we travel,
- who we elect to office,
- the letters we write concerning Bread for the World and other similar causes,
- and how we cry out against abuses and waste in the system.

We must share our abundance and we can care with a conscience. For caring leads to creative action.

So we need to be continually open to the words of Saint Paul: "So let us not grow weary in doing what is right, for we will reap at harvest-time, if we do not give up" (Galatians 6:9).

How To Celebrate
A Church Anniversary

Every church, in one way or another, was assisted in the birth process by the generosity of others. Along with denominational assistance, local church history often records expressions of generosity not only from members but from neighbors and others who themselves had no church connection. And the records often show that sister churches gave support in many ways: new members, communionware, hymn books, pulpit furnishings, and other essential items along with strong financial support. All of these gifts represent the whole process of "passing along blessings."

Through the years it has been the custom in many churches to take a special offering at an anniversary celebration. Uses have varied but often all or a substantial part of such offerings has been used for mission projects. This is an exciting way to celebrate an anniversary and to pass along an expression of thanks, particularly if it in any way contributes to the rebirth of a declining congregation or the beginning of a new church development. A new church is evangelism in action and can be the enhanced extension of an existing church's outreach. Although an anniversary is a time of church family-sharing and renewal it can also give evidence that "the mark of a living church is the size of its benevolent heart."

Statements/Reminders/ Mission Interpreters

Most churches send out statements or reminders on a periodic basis: monthly, quarterly, annually. A statement can be just that — the amount of one's pledge and payments made to date. We are all used to statements or, more euphemistically speaking, "reminders." They are a necessary way of doing business in an increasingly complex world. We dread them at times and they can make us feel very uncomfortable. Seldom do we rejoice when they arrive in the mail. They tell us that we owe something or that we are indebted to someone.

However, many businesses have made the most of the advantage of getting into our homes. Not only do they indicate we owe something, but many businesses are using statements for advertising as well. Along with the form indicating what we owe and the time limits for payment we are deluged by many colorful flyers telling us about sensational bargains or when the next sale is to begin. We may not like what we owe, but at the same time we may be intrigued by new bargain possibilities.

The church statement/reminder needs to be viewed, not as a necessary evil, but as a positive stewardship tool. People have voluntarily made a pledge to the church and the reminder shows where they are in keeping current with that pledge. But it can also be used as an expression of thanks. We do not do enough thanking in the church and here is one way we can say thanks in a different way every time reminders are sent. More importantly, the reminders should inform the members about ways in which their money is being used. Every statement/reminder can tell a story of people being helped, some good being accomplished, new work being started, lives being enriched because someone cares. The statement should be a message of good news. That's what the gospel is about and stewardship is putting the gospel in action.

Members of the Stewardship and Mission Committee should work with the church treasurer or whoever is responsible for mailing the pledge payment information. And a different message should be formulated for each mailing. An informed congregation keeps giving generously when people know how their gifts are used to make a difference. In addition, statement/reminders may carry special news about congregational events, church activities, concerts, and programs. Let the church's message carry positive news!

Stewardship Season Humor

A young minister was preaching his first sermon. He was preaching from the book of Revelation on the text: "Behold, I come quickly and my reward is with me." He began his sermon with the text saying, "Behold, I come ..." then drew a blank and could think of nothing more to say. He tried again, "Behold, I come ..." Nothing happened. Dull silence. Finally, he cleared his throat, took a deep breath and shouted with renewed energy, "Behold, I come ..." and in leaning forward, the pulpit gave way and he tumbled from the platform and landed in the lap of a little old day in the front row. As he looked up at her, in chagrin, he apologized profusely. But she simply smiled back and said: "No need to apologize, young man. I can't say you didn't give me fair warning." The stewardship season is part of the rhythm of church life. Fair warning is always given, with no need for apology.

* * * * *

Martin Luther was reputed to have said that every person needs two conversions: the conversion of the heart and the conversion of the pocketbook. Generally speaking, most pastors would agree that the conversion of the heart usually comes about much more easily than the conversion of the pocketbook.

* * * * *

There is the story of the banker who moved to a small town where he would serve as the president of the local bank. The first Sunday he attended church it happened to be a campaign Sunday to gather pledges for a new educational building. The banker felt he should do something so he made a conservative pledge of $100.

He was flabbergasted when he read the headline of the weekly church newsletter gushing forth the news that Banker Jones had pledged $10,000 for the new building. A slight problem with a decimal point. He called the pastor and explained the amount of his pledge but finally conceded that it would be difficult for everyone concerned if the amount was changed. He agreed to give the whole amount with the stipulation, however, that he would provide the inscription over the door to the building. The pastor was agreeable as long as it was biblical. The banker assured him that it would be.

So the day came when the building was to be dedicated. A great crowd had gathered and there was a drapery over the door, above which was the dedication. After the proper ceremonies, the banker was asked to pull the cord on the drapery, which he did. And there was the inscription for all the world to see: "I was a stranger, and you took me in."

* * * * *

There is a story about a clergyman in a small community who would leave town every day at 5:00. He was so consistent in his exodus that the local gossips became curious. After months had passed a parishioner finally found the courage to ask the preacher where he went every day at 5:00. The young minister replied: "Every day as eventide comes I get into my car and drive down to the railroad track and wait. Then at ten minutes past 5:00 the train goes by. I sigh and say to myself, "Thank heaven, there goes something I don't have to push!" (*Appropriate for some pastors to use at stewardship time.*)

* * * * *

Author Rufus Jones tells a delightful story about a blacksmith in a small Maine town. The blacksmith was so extremely short of stature that he was very humble-minded. He fell deeply in love with the tallest and fairest girl in the village, but he did not dare to tell her of his love, and for years he kept the secret locked in his heart.

One day, however, the girl came into his shop to have something made. He pounded it out for her on the anvil, and she was so warmly appreciative that then and there he proposed to her. She accepted him on the spot, and leaping on his anvil he kissed her heartily. Then he asked her to take a walk with him, which she did. After a suitable time he asked if he might kiss her again, but she refused. "Not here in public," she said. "Well, then," he replied, "if there isn't going to be any more kissing, I'm not going to carry this anvil any farther. It's heavy."

Life is not all kissing. It is more often carrying anvils. The things to which we commit ourselves are often costly enterprises. But we must stand on the anvil of commitment in order to kiss the glory of attainment.

www.ingramcontent.com/pod-product-compliance
Lightning Source LLC
Chambersburg PA
CBHW071724090426
42738CB00009B/1868